Sales Closing For Dummies®

BESTSELLING BOOK SERIES

Cheat Sheet

Buying Signs

- Asking general questions.
- Asking specific, technical questions.
- Intently reading brochures or other materials.
- Verbal assents such as "uh-huh," "hmm," and "I see."
- Leaning forward.
- Relaxing.
- Smiling.
- Showing affection, touching, or holding hands.
- Touching the product.
- Measuring the dimensions for fit.
- Speeding up the buying pace.
- Slowing down the buying pace.

Closing Tough Customers

1. Acknowledge your customer's anger.
2. Stay calm.
3. Clear your mind of all other clients.
4. Make it clear that you are sincerely concerned.
5. Don't hurry your client.
6. Adopt a what-have-I-got-to-lose attitude. (Don't confuse this with a devil-may-care attitude.)
7. Stay interested in the client's needs and his situation.
8. Understand *why* your customer feels out of control in the buying process.
9. Ask questions — get the customer talking about solutions.
10. Acknowledge the probablity of a "worst-case scenario," your losing your client. Do everything to prevent it.

For Dummies: Bestselling Book Series for Beginners

BESTSELLING
BOOK SERIES

Sales Closing For Dummies®

Cheat Sheet

Reasons for Buying Products or Services

- The customer wants his needs fulfilled.
- Your product keeps up with the times.
- Your product stays ahead of competition.
- Your product is the biggest.
- Your product can be applied to both large and small business needs.
- Your product makes the customer feel secure.
- Your product is well-respected throughout its market.
- Your product feeds the customer's vanity.
- Your product brings status.
- Your product is appropriate for a season or event.
- The customer is compulsive.

Reasons for Not Buying Products or Services

- Your product fails to meet the customers' needs.
- Your product doesn't stand out.
- The customer procrastinates.
- The customer doesn't want to spend money on your product.
- Your product is not marketed well.
- The customer doesn't trust you or your product.
- The customer has had a bad experience in the past
- The customer is indecisive.
- Your product's timing is poor.
- The customer is happy with her current supplier.
- You never asked the customer for the sale.

For Dummies: Bestselling Book Series for Beginners

Praise for Sales Closing For Dummies

"Tom Hopkins teaches his most advanced students that Sales Champions are masters of the fundamentals. In *Sales Closing For Dummies,* Tom beautifully and thoroughly describes those fundamentals with his familiar 'Red Flag' key points and situation scripts — Tom clearly reminds us that professional selling is about communication, not coercion."

> — Michael Tove, District Sales Trainer, CMA

"Without a doubt, this is the most revolutionary book you will ever read on selling successfully. Tom Hopkins' wisdom has created boundless wealth in the lives of salespeople around the world."

> — Glenna Salsbury, CSP, CPAE, President of the
> National Speakers Association 1997–98,
> Author of *The Art of the Fresh Start*

"Tom Hopkins always stands at the front gates of progress, holding up the cue-cards for eager-beaver sales stars. *Sales Closing For Dummies,* his latest sales closing book, contains practical, how-to oriented, ready-to-apply ideas that any sales professional can use to close more sales and build competition-proof relationships."

> — Gerhard Gschwandtner, Publisher,
> *Selling Power Magazine*

"Tom Hopkins' sincerity and clarity permeate every page. His strategies empower me to defeat anything that defies success, not only in sales but in life."

> — Judith Ann Roberts, Personal Financial Analyst,
> Primerica Financial Services

"In this easy-to-read book, Tom Hopkins, the master salesman, teaches you how to overcome objections, create a sense of urgency, and then close the sale. As founder of the largest woman-owned business in Arizona, I've learned the importance of locking up the sale. This clear, concise book empowers you to close more sales and put money in the bank."

> — Linda Brock-Nelson, Former Owner/Founder,
> Linda Brock Auto Mall

"In *Sales Closing For Dummies,* Tom demystifies the mysteries about how to close — you'll discover that closing the sale is not a trap you set but a process that evolves effortlessly."

> — Danielle Kennedy, author of *Seven Figure Selling*
> and *Balancing Acts — An Inspirational Guide for
> Working Mothers*

More Praise for Sales Closing For Dummies

"Finally, this basic, fundamental information from the master, Tom Hopkins, is available. If you are serious about becoming the best you can be in sales, this is a must-have book! Make sure everyone you know in sales gets this book. This information, when followed, will increase your bottom line. It will work for you. Your future will be brighter, better, and more prosperous when you practice, drill, and rehearse this information. Here is the map of how to close the sale. Pay attention. I am so thankful I did."

> — Jan Ruhe, Author and Music Producer, World Class Sales/Training/Marketing Master, www.fireup.com

"I loved this book — and I hate to read! This book will help rookies and veterans alike learn how to sell to the customer of the '90s. Fun and easy to read, it's a must for anyone whose goal is incredible success."

> — Ken BrockBank, Vice President, Unishippers

"Tom Hopkins' *Sales Closing For Dummies* is packed with so many great ideas for selling, I find myself highlighting every page. It's highly informative and entertaining to read."

> — Robert L. Shook, Author of more than 40 books including *The Greatest Sales Stories Ever Told*

"Our readers look forward to Tom Hopkins' articles because of his ability to explain and illustrate his famous champion selling strategies so that salespeople can easily understand and apply them to increase their own sales. In this book, he incorporates the *For Dummies* practical learning style to make all of his successful professional selling strategies even easier to acquire."

> — Homer Smith, Editor of *Master Salesmanship*

"Tom Hopkins is the foremost authority today in the field and subject of sales closing. Not since the days of J. Douglas Edwards has there been someone as astute in this art as Tom Hopkins. This masterpiece of information will open new vistas and great horizons for all who read it. It is a must-read for everyone who desires the best that life can offer."

> — Larry W. Coyle, Executive Vice President, TeamUp International, Inc.

"So often, salespeople meet qualified clients only to lose them in the end. Closing is nothing more than the ability to gain agreement. This straightforward book provides all the dialog you could possibly need."

> — Diane Turton, Diane Turton Realtors

"If you're new to sales, this is definitely the book to read. If you are an experienced sales professional, there's plenty of good, solid advice and tips for you, too. Tom Hopkins is a master sales trainer whose vast experience is shared with you in an easy-to-understand-and-then-use manner."

— Louis O. Sepulveda, C.P.P.

"All the work, all the rejection, all the planning — *all* go down the drain until you figure out how to close the sale eloquently, and who better to teach you than the master, Tom Hopkins. *Sales Closing For Dummies* gives everyone from the beginner to the seasoned pro insights that are necessary to reach true professionalism in the art of selling."

— Dave Ramsey, Author of *New York Times* Bestseller, *Financial Peace*

"*Sales Closing For Dummies* is amazingly detailed, with each step choreographed in how to close every sale. I've torn apart and reengineered the material to fit marketing romance. This book has given me the right words to say to portray an image of professionalism and competence, create trust, and close sales. It contains hundreds of fresh-sounding sales questions and responses with examples from an impressive cross-section of industries. It's like tapping into your own private panel of sales experts. I can't afford not to read this book and have it in my library."

— Roseann Higgins, President & Founder, S.P.I.E.S.

"This is a classic — clear, concise, and filled with powerful principles that anyone can use to become a top-producing sales person. I know: Over the course of my seventeen-year financial consulting career, I've applied Tom's proven sales strategies and have benefited greatly as a result. I know of many others — sales professionals from all walks of life — who have enjoyed new levels of success by applying the insights in this informative book. If you want to increase your sales, read *Sales Closing For Dummies* now."

— E. Anthony Reguero, ChFC, Chartered Financial Consultant

"*Sales Closing For Dummies* is a must-read for everyone who has committed him or herself to sales as a profession. Tom has distilled his years of experience into a format that is challenging, and provides techniques that are easily applied. I strongly encourage you to put its proven methods to use today!"

— Chuck Burtzloff, President & CEO of Cardservice International, Inc.

More Praise for Sales Closing For Dummies

"A precise, step-by-step, easy to understand sales manual which teaches and inspires the novice, while sharpening the skills of the lifelong sales professional. A book to be referred to over and over again by a master of sales."

—Laura Laaman, Sales Speaker and Author

"This is a great book for the beginner and old pro as well. The ideas and techniques that Tom shares in this book will help all sales-people to increase sales and that's the bottom line."

—Ed Callaghan, President, National Training Corporation of America

 TM

References for the Rest of Us!™

SALES CLOSING FOR DUMMIES®

by Tom Hopkins

Wiley Publishing, Inc.

Sales Closing For Dummies®

Published by
Wiley Publishing, Inc.
111 River Street
Hoboken, NJ 07030
www.wiley.com

Copyright © 1998 Tom Hopkins International, Inc.
Published by Wiley Publishing, Inc., Indianapolis, Indiana
Published simultaneously in Canada

For general information on our other products and services or to obtain technical support, please contact our Customer Care Department within the U.S. at 800-762-2974, outside the U.S. at 317-572-3993, or fax 317-572-4002.

Wiley also publishes its books in a variety of electronic formats. Some content that appears in print may not be available in electronic books.

Library of Congress Cataloging-in-Publication Data:

Library of Congress Control Number: 98-84648

ISBN: 0-7645-5063-2

Manufactured in the United States of America

15 14 13 12 11

1O/TR/RQ/QV/IN

About the Author

Tom Hopkins is the epitome of sales success. A millionaire by the time he reached the age of 27, Hopkins is now chairman of Tom Hopkins International, the largest sales training organization in the world. Each year, he teaches professional selling skills to hundreds of thousands of students around the world.

Thirty-four years ago, Tom Hopkins considered himself a failure. He had dropped out of college after 90 days and for the next 18 months, he carried steel on construction sites to make a living. Believing that there had to be a better way to earn a living, he went into sales — and ran into the worst period of his life. For six months, Hopkins earned an average of $42 per month and slid deeper into debt and despair. Pulling together his last few dollars, he invested in a three-day sales training seminar that turned his life around. In the next six months, Hopkins sold more than $1 million worth of $25,000 homes.

At age 21, he won the Los Angeles Sales and Marketing Institute's coveted SAMMY Award and began setting records in sales performance that still stand today.

Because of his unique ability to share his enthusiasm for the profession of selling and the selling techniques he developed, Hopkins began giving seminars in 1974. Training as many as 10,000 salespeople a month, he quickly became known as the world's leading sales trainer.

He was a pioneer in producing high-quality audio and video-tape programs for those who could not attend the seminars or who wanted further reinforcement after the seminars. Recognized as the most effective sales training programs ever produced, they are continually updated and are now being utilized by more than 1 million people.

Tom Hopkins has also written ten books, including the best-selling *How to Master the Art of Selling,* which has sold over 1.3 million copies in nine languages and three *For Dummies* books: *Selling For Dummies, Sales Prospecting For Dummies,* and now this book, *Sales Closing For Dummies.*

Hopkins is a member of the National Speakers Association and one of a select few to ever receive its Council of Peers Award for Excellence. He is often the keynote speaker for annual conventions and is a frequent guest on television and radio talk shows.

Dedication

This book is dedicated to the person who said "yes" to my greatest sale ever. Her name is Debbie Hopkins, my beloved wife, confidante, and friend. She has taught me volumes on how to love, live, and laugh. For the last 20 years, she has truly been the wind beneath my wings that enabled me to fly high and thus achieve the fulfillment of my dreams.

My greatest sale ever was getting the "yes" she gave when I asked her to become my wife.

Author's Acknowledgments

First and foremost, I acknowledge my lovely bride, Debbie, for giving me valuable input and feedback on all of my books, especially this one, which we worked on while "on vacation."

I thank John Kilcullen, Hungry Minds CEO, for his friendship, his support of our training, and his dedication to making the *For Dummies* books what they are today — an invaluable resource for the general public on just about any topic you can imagine. Good going, John.

I thank Kathy Welton and Mark Butler of Hungry Minds for getting the ball rolling on this book and on *Sales Prospecting For Dummies*. Should we have a Cross Reference icon here, guys?

Thanks also go to Judy Slack, my Director of Research & Development, for translating our material into the *For Dummies* style and researching the new content that was needed.

Special thanks go out to one of the finest sales professionals I know, Olivia Woolsey, for the hours spent reviewing the material to ensure that it meets the needs of today's top people.

And thanks go to Debi Siegel, the writer who worked with all of us at THI, for putting together the first draft so we could all tear it up and fine tune it into what you now hold in your hands.

Last, but not least, I thank Tere Drenth and Andrea Boucher, our editors at Hungry Minds, for their diligence in keeping everything on schedule and up to the *For Dummies* standards.

Publisher's Acknowledgments

We're proud of this book; please register your comments through our online registration form located at: www.dummies.com/register.

Some of the people who helped bring this book to market include the following:

Acquisitions, Development, and Editorial

Project Editor: Tere Drenth

Acquisitions Editor: Mark Butler

Copy Editor: Andrea C. Boucher

General Reviewer: Olivia Woolsey

Editorial Manager: Elaine Brush

Editorial Coordinator: Maureen F. Kelly

Acquisitions Assistant: Nickole Harris

Composition

Project Coordinator: E. Shawn Aylsworth

Layout and Graphics: Cameron Booker, Lou Boudreau, Linda Boyer, J. Tyler Connor, Kelly Hardesty, Angela F. Hunckler, Jane E. Martin, Anna Rohrer, Brent Savage, Janet Seib, Kate Snell

Proofreaders: Christine Berman, Kelli Botta, Michelle Croninger, Rachel Garvey, Arielle Carole Menelle, Rebecca Senninger, Janet M. Withers

Indexer: Ann Norcross

Publishing and Editorial for Consumer Dummies

Diane Graves Steele, Vice President and Publisher, Consumer Dummies

Joyce Pepple, Acquisitions Director, Consumer Dummies

Kristin A. Cocks, Product Development Director, Consumer Dummies

Michael Spring, Vice President and Publisher, Travel

Brice Gosnell, Publishing Director, Travel

Suzanne Jannetta, Editorial Director, Travel

Publishing for Technology Dummies

Richard Swadley, Vice President and Executive Group Publisher

Andy Cummings, Vice President and Publisher

Composition Services

Gerry Fahey, Vice President of Production Services

Debbie Stailey, Director of Composition Services

Contents at a Glance

Cartoons at a Glance

By Rich Tennant

Cartoon Information:
Fax: 978-546-7747
E-Mail: richtennant@the5thwave.com
World Wide Web: www.the5thwave.com

Table of Contents

Introduction

*T*here are many steps in a professional selling cycle, from
locating and meeting prospective clients to qualifying,
demonstrating, and addressing concerns to the final closing of
the sale. I cover each of these steps in great detail in *Selling For
Dummies* (Hungry Minds, Inc.). After receiving feedback from
readers of *Selling For Dummies* and from students attending my
seminars, I decided that what sales professionals are really
seeking are answers on sales closing.

Closing is the be all and end all in selling. Getting the approval on
the dotted line is the brass ring — it's the big payoff, the win.
Closing on the final agreement is the number one goal of everyone who is involved in selling a product, service, or idea to
another individual or company (which is why there's such a high
level of interest in this subject).

Many salespeople walk away from a non-sale situation feeling
defeated, wondering what they could have done differently to
close the sale. Unfortunately, these defeated salespeople often
don't invest the time in surveying prospective clients about why
they didn't make the purchase. Ew! Doesn't that sound awkward?
But you need to know answers to questions like this.

The thing I find most interesting is that when you do ask clients
why they chose not to own your product, many of them state that
they were never asked! They were never asked? What kind of
salesperson goes through all the other steps and then doesn't
even ask for the sale? The answer: salespeople of every type.

One of our greatest fears as humans is to be thought of poorly —
to be rejected. Unfortunately, that single fear has kept millions of
people from becoming high achievers in the field of selling. Many
of those people have given up on selling and are living lives
where their financial incomes are dictated (limited?) by someone
else. And that's too bad, because it doesn't have to be this way.

For you, the person who is dedicated enough to pick up a copy of
this book, don't give up. The answers to many of your questions
lie here in the pages, waiting to be read.

In fact, my goal in this book is to help you gain a solid perspective on what closing is, what it does for all the parties involved,
and some simple yet powerful ways to ask people for their
commitment to your product or service. And the more comfortable you are, the more comfortable your customers will be.

Who Should Read This Book

This book is written with the traditional salesperson in mind. By traditional, I mean someone who earns his or her living primarily from moving products or services into the lives of end-users.

- ✔ It's for you — if you find yourself hesitating to ask for the sale.

- ✔ It's for you — if you have ever walked away from a sale because your enthusiastic clients didn't jump up and say, "We'll take it" and immediately reach for their checkbook.

- ✔ It's for you — if you've already read *Selling For Dummies* but want more information on closing.

- ✔ It's for you — if you're a career salesperson who wants to boost his or her closing ratio.

- ✔ It's for you — if you're a small business person struggling to grow your business, whether it's business with suppliers or clients.

- ✔ It's for you — if you're involved in network marketing and find that sharing the products and opportunities aren't helping you build your organization as quickly as you'd like. We cover strategies for persuading others to get involved in your organization or to try your products.

All the material found within these pages is based on over 30 years of personal experience and research, the experience of top professionals in many fields, and sound psychological principles. Everything I discuss has been proven to work in the real world of selling.

How to Use This Book

Although it's likely that you'll be drawn first to the chapters full of closes and phraseology in Part II, or get a highlight of the strategies in the Parts of Tens, I strongly recommend that you eventually read all of Part I in order to gain a clear understanding of the psychology behind what's happening when you attempt to close a sale. I also recommend that you read this book with a highlighter handy. Highlight the points that are most meaningful or pertinent to you on your first read. In doing so, you've turned this great little textbook into a handy quick reference guide.

This book is small enough to tag along with you in your briefcase. However, I don't recommend you leave it there for long. The best place for this book is in your hands, open to the very piece of information you need to help you close your next sale.

As you read through the book, you'll find that I use several different terms for the salesperson (you) and for the client. So that you won't be confused, here's a listing of the various terms I use:

Salesperson	Client
Sales professional	Prospect
Expert	Future client
Mr./Ms. Sales Expert	Non-client
Mr./Ms. Salesperson	Prospective client
Champion	Customer
Top producer	Unclient
You	Them
Master closer	Decision maker
Superstar closer	Professional shopper

How This Book Is Organized

Sales Closing For Dummies is organized into four parts. Here are the parts of the book and what they contain:

Part I: A Close by Any Other Name Is Still a Close

This part goes into detail on what closing really is. (Hint: Closing isn't just getting a signature on the dotted line and a check.) I define closing, tear it apart into small, digestible pieces, and then put it back together again. By reading this part, you find out about the emotions your prospective clients go through in making decisions and how to use that knowledge to your advantage.

Part II: Tactics and Strategies of Champion Closers

Here's the meat of the book: It's the what-to-say and how-to-say-it part. Part II is where you find specific closes with their proven successful phraseology, which you can master and begin using right away. I also include situations in which each close works best.

Part III: Continuing to Build Your Business

In this part, I go over methods for maximizing business with every close. The methods I discuss include strategies to keep your clients' business and develop loyalty, build on your first sale to earn ongoing business, and when and how to bow out gracefully if their needs no longer meet yours (or vice versa).

Part IV: The Part of Tens

The brief chapters in this part are filled with ideas for closing that you can implement quickly and easily into your current selling style. The Part of Tens also covers closing mistakes to avoid, reasons why people do or don't buy your product, and how to make your customers comfortable. These chapters take only a few minutes to read and are a great way to get yourself pumped up for a sales call.

Icons in This Book

 In this case, a red flag is a good thing! This icon marks little slogans that you, as a salesperson, can say to yourself to keep yourself motivated.

 This icon marks personal stories that I've acquired through my years of experience in selling, as well as the experience of my students.

 Want to know exactly what to say in a situation? Look for these icons — they represent actual scripts and strategies that have been proven effective in many selling situations.

 This is the "Salesperson Beware" icon. This icon alerts you to situations that can turn a customer off or cause you to lose the sale.

 This icon denotes specific closing methods and the situations in which each works best.

The items marked by this icon are important to your overall image as a professional in this business. Try to commit them to memory, so that you act on them naturally.

This icon helps you find even more valuable information on the topic at hand in either *Selling For Dummies* or *Sales Prospecting For Dummies.*

Where to Go from Here

Anywhere inside this book. I've tried to make every page count. Each page is geared to contain at least one practical piece of information to assist you in improving your closing ratio and serving more clients. I want you to be comfortable with the material, so please begin wherever you feel most comfortable.

Part I

A Close by Any Other Name Is Still a Close

The 5th Wave   By Rich Tennant

Auto Parts

"I worked at a dealership, but always choked on the closing. Somehow, selling cars a part at a time seems easier."

In this part . . .

*I*n this part, I dissect closing into palatable, bite-sized pieces to help you quickly digest what it's all about. Hopefully, you'll start to love closing as much as the top producers around the world do and begin to master the traits of top closers, which I cover in Chapter 3.

Chapter 1

Falling in Love with Closing

....

....

I love selling! If you love it, too, you're nodding your head in agreement to that statement, and you're well on your way to becoming a great success in the sales industry. One of the first things you have to do in this business is to fall in love with selling; selling is not something you can be somewhat so-so about.

When you love sales, you automatically think about it all the time. Selling is more like a hobby than a job or even a career. To illustrate my point, suppose gardening is your hobby. You simply love to garden. You have a garden. You have books about gardening. You think about gardening when you come home. You work on your garden every spare moment you have. In other words, gardening gives you great pleasure. Because you love gardening so much, you study it. You read about plants, their cycles, proper nourishment, and even lighting requirements. Before too long, you know almost everything there is to know about gardening. In fact, you're building quite a reputation in the neighborhood for being an expert gardener. Now think of sales in terms of a hobby. When you love sales, your hobby — what you truly enjoy doing — is your livelihood. And who wouldn't want that?

To become a top producer in the sales field, you have to devote time and attention to selling — like you do with a hobby. Just as a gardener watches and studies his plants, you have to study your customers.

✔ Examine their emotions.

Become aware of any fears they have regarding decision-making (selling) situations. Refer to Chapter 6 to find out more about fear in selling situations.

✔ Observe them in everyday buying and selling situations.

✔ Recognize buying signs and behaviors.

People act a certain way when they're interested enough to make a purchase. I cover this in detail in Chapter 2.

You're constantly selling and constantly moving toward a close. Either you're closing your prospective customer on the idea of owning your offering, or they're closing you on the idea of taking your presentation and moving on to somebody who cares (that is, they just flat aren't interested). If you want your selling situations to be more like the first scenario, become an excellent student of human nature.

Covering Your Bases

Sales closing is the brass ring of selling, the climax, the bottom line. If you covered all your bases to the point of closing the selling situation, the close itself should go as smooth as silk. By covering all your bases, I mean you've properly handled all the following steps, which come before closing in the selling cycle:

✔ **Prospecting:** Finding the people to sell.

✔ **Original contact:** Making a positive first impression.

✔ **Qualification:** Determining if this person has the need and ability to own.

✔ **Presentation:** Demonstrating your product effectively.

Each of these steps is covered in my book, *Selling For Dummies* — if you're looking for a great overall selling skills book, this is the one you need. Prospecting is covered in great depth in another of my books, *Sales Prospecting For Dummies* (both by IDG Books Worldwide, Inc.).

What Is the Selling Process without Closing?

Without closing, the selling process isn't much. After all, why go into sales if you aren't going to practice closing? I hate to say it, but you're wasting your time and that of your prospective customers if you don't close. Presenting without closing is like a story with no ending. Or worse yet, it's a story that you know has a great ending, but the storyteller stops just before the end and refuses to tell the rest. Instead of remembering all the fun of the story, you walk away angry and frustrated.

Without a close, everybody loses. Believe me when I tell you that your prospective customers don't want to have wasted their time. They want to own, so let them. And obviously, you don't want to have spent hours preparing for the call and not close, right? Your company doesn't want to have invested money and time in your training to have you do everything right until it comes to the close and then walk out. Lastly, your family doesn't want to see you frustrated and suffer the financial loses that come with the inability to close a transaction. So decide to be a winner and let all those involved in the transaction win, too. All you have to do is ask for the business and close the sale.

Closing is the easiest thing to do when you've done everything else right; it's the most difficult thing to do when you've botched the rest of your presentation. Although you do come across a great closer and a weak presenter every now and then, it's more common to see great presenters and weak closers. Just remember, nobody benefits from owning or selling if you can't or won't close.

Tom's Definition of Closing

Figuring out when, where, or how to close a transaction is difficult if you have no true understanding of what closing is all about. Closing means different things to different people.

- ✔ For some, it's simply taking an order or ringing up a sale on the cash register.

- ✔ For others, closing is the culmination of hours spent re-searching, planning, presenting, questioning, persuading, discovering, and finally helping the prospective buyer to own your offering.

For me, closing has been an evolutionary process of realization that without professional, expert help, many customers would not be fortunate enough to benefit from owning my product or service. Because I believe in my product so completely, it doesn't make sense to hold back the opportunity for others to enjoy the advantages of ownership. Thirty years in this business have taught me, firsthand, how to be a natural, helpful, skilled closer who cares enough to help his prospective clients own.

Closing can be defined in the following ways:

- ✔ A well-filled ink pen in the hands of a sane, mature individual who affixes a signature to a predetermined dotted line with no physical help from the salesperson.

  Doesn't this paint an interesting picture? Yes, that pen better be filled with ink. The clients must be competent to make a decision and we, as salespeople, cannot physically move them to approve the paperwork.

✔ Professionally using a person's desire to own the benefits of your product and then blending your sincere desire to serve in helping a person make a decision that's truly good for them.

Now I'm talking service. The clients do have a desire to own or they wouldn't invest their valuable time talking with you, right? You must have a sincere desire to help them and serve their needs. And most importantly, the decision to own must be truly good for them.

What kind of a night's sleep would you get tonight if you helped a young couple make a decision to own a home that you knew was beyond their means — even if they wanted it? If you're dedicated to being a professional, you wouldn't sleep well at all. If you're truly a professional, you would help them find another home that they could fall in love with — and afford.

✔ A symphony of words and actions that emotionally build, culminating with a win/win final agreement.

This view of selling is the definitive mark for the people that I train today.

The word "symphony" was written within this definition for a reason. Today we listen to classical music composed centuries ago with as much awe and inspiration as when it was first performed. I look at a natural close exactly the same way. I listen to the words that build and culminate into an emotional finish, a symphony of words that tugs at the heartstrings of our customers until they know they just have to enter into the win/win situation of owning my product or service. I win if the customers own my product; they win because they are gaining tremendous benefits that they'll enjoy for years to come. The symphony comes into play when all those minor agreements build emotionally into a melody of culminating win/win notes designed to move everybody involved toward the common goal of closing.

What closing is not

Oftentimes, it's easier to describe and get a clear picture of what something is by knowing what it is not. By the same token, I thought it would be helpful to first of all let you know what closing is *not* before I tell you what it *is*. So, closing is not:

✔ **Comfortable (in the beginning)**

Closing will be extremely uncomfortable for you at times, and I won't promise that it gets a whole lot better the tenth time you attempt to close. However, the more successes you experience, the more eager you will be to accept those "nos" and turn them into "yeses."

✔ **Magical**

I think this is probably the most misunderstood aspect of closing. Some would have you believe that what they do is mystical and magical and that the ability to close is something you either have or you don't have. Not so — don't believe a word of it. Everyone has the ability to be a competent, even talented closer. A certain personality type doesn't close better than another. I've seen a very reserved, almost introverted salesperson be an incredible closer, so that certainly isn't the case. And the good closers aren't always the 20-year veterans who have cornered the market on closing. I've also seen a two-month rookie close with the best of them. Closing involves no magic and there's no mystery to it — just determination to be successful at your craft.

What closing is

Okay. So you know what closing isn't. Here's what it is:

✔ **An art**

Although closing isn't magical, there is an art to it. Every word you say is creating an image, either from memory or from experience, be it your approach, interview, presentation, questioning, value building, or closing. You are constructing a picture with your words, and what you are attempting to do is get your customers to catch your vision. How? Well, you appeal to their senses. You build and build and build the vision and excitement until the customers are emotionally peaked to own.

✔ **Enhanced by practice**

Boy, is that low-tech or what? Many have the knowledge and skill to close a transaction but don't implement what they know. The bad thing about closing is that it's difficult to practice without doing so on live customers. You have to take a chance and make yourself ask for the business, make yourself close. Don't worry that it isn't the right time, place, or person — just keep closing. The more you close, the more you develop your closing instinct.

ANECDOTE

The art of closing

I love art. About 12 years ago when I first started collecting art, I would look at some of the masters like Picasso, Dali, Miro, and I'd say to myself, "Wow, is that ever ugly!" You see, in the beginning I had no appreciation of art. Then I began to study the greats and I realized that the images on canvas came from images and feelings based on knowledge, past experiences, and learned skills of the artists.

Every word you say is just like taking a canvas and starting to paint pictures in the person's mind. All the right words create the right pictures based on their buying motivation. The wrong words create something that they don't enjoy seeing — fear, which is the greatest enemy in the art of closing. You know what? You're not in the business of selling; you're in the business of people, and moving them to own by painting word pictures is an unbelievably important part of your business.

✔ **Natural**

Closing should be a logical move, a natural progression to the final step of the selling process. You may be saying, "Tom, closing isn't natural for me at all!" Okay, I hear you. Because closing doesn't feel natural now doesn't mean that it'll never feel natural; it means that you need to figure out what you're doing right when closing *does* feel natural — and continue to do more of the same.

✔ **Fun**

Okay, now I may be stretching it a bit for some of you, but I believe successfully closing a sale is very fun. I've met especially challenging prospects before and persuaded them to get happily involved in my product and/or service. When they decided to own, I walked away about ten feet off the ground — it was a kick! Closing is fun. Now, I'll agree that attempting to close and not closing isn't a lot of fun, and that's where the frustration can come in. Keep practicing. I promise you, all the practice and effort will be worth your time when you experience the fun of a great close.

✔ **Always possible**

I'm sure you've heard that there are some people who just can't be closed. Not true! We all want to own; we just don't want to buy. If you have successfully set up an appointment with clients, they want to own what you're offering. They can be closed. Maybe not on the first visit, and maybe not by you, but they can be closed when the time is right. Even though there are temporary conditions to a sale that may prevent the customer from owning now, it's your job to try to remove those obstacles and close the sale. If you never try to close, I can guarantee you that you'll be the warm-up act for the next salesperson who isn't afraid to ask for the business.

Do You Have to Go through All the Closing Steps?

Sometimes you do — sometimes you don't! Whether you have to go through every closing step depends on the customers and your ability to create an emotional experience. If you've done a great job and you're halfway through your presentation when

Bulldog determination

I'm not ashamed to admit it. The first few years I was in the business, many salespeople who were lucky enough to get my prospects after I thought they couldn't be closed were thanking me all the way to the bank. I remember being so frustrated when I saw this happen. The difference between me and many other salespeople who got out of the business is that I was determined to learn every element of sales and master them one by one. I was devoted to success and determined to close.

Determination is what it takes to be a successful closer — that "bulldog"

determination that you're going to learn to close and get comfortable with the process no matter what. Until you do become a strong closer, you're really nothing but an interesting conversationalist. Don't get me wrong; when I say *strong closer* I don't mean that you must be that obnoxious, rowdy stereotypical salesperson. I mean that you have to stay focused on your objective, and your objective should always be to close. Whether you're closing for the appointment, closing on building rapport and a relationship, or closing on the sale, stay focused and keep closing.

your prospects begin giving you buying signs (see Chapter 2), attempt to close them right then and there. In this case, if you stick to going through all the steps, you may cause them to cool down and change their minds. The danger of skipping some of the steps is when you take shortcuts that prevent your prospects from seeing the fuller picture of your offering.

The more you close, the more you realize that each situation is different, which is what makes selling and closing so much fun. Every day presents a new challenge. Every transaction enables the salesperson to practice different skills and closing strategies. Every success paves the way for more successes. Closing becomes more powerful, more effective, and more efficient the more you successfully close.

Why Is Closing a Dirty Word to Some People?

We are constantly playing off old experiences that may have taught us to fear, to inaccurately judge or to mistakenly act. Some of our experiences are so strong that the images they have created in our minds are almost impossible to erase. Notice I said *almost* impossible. For some of us, it takes a lot more work to become strong closers because we have to erase the concept that "closing" is a dirty word.

For me, I had to get over thinking of closing as a bad word. My parents taught me never to ask others for things. Asking for something wasn't polite; consequently, asking for business was very difficult for me to do. I'd go out and give a powerful presentation; I'd spend hours building rapport, establishing trust and confidence in my ability to do the job; then I'd leave without asking the prospects to own. In fact, I didn't even realize that I wasn't asking for the sale.

So, right now, I'd like to give all of you who were raised like me permission to ask others for the business. Here's how I would suggest you get over this hesitation to ask: Reinforce the idea that you are not really *asking* for something from others; you are *offering* something to them. Now, wouldn't your parents be upset with you if you had company in your home and didn't offer them refreshments? Okay, think of closing as the same thing. If you take up a prospect's time and fail to offer him anything in return, you're not being fair to him, are you? Does this help you change your attitude about asking? Thinking of closing in terms of offering sure helped me!

Closing is also considered a dirty word because of the feelings it can sometimes conjure up in both the salesperson and his or her prospective customer. If you've attempted to close and you haven't done a great job of things, you've probably helped to create a fearful or uncomfortable situation. Perhaps you've been pushy or came across looking too eager or anxious, and your customers lost trust in you. Or maybe you did a fairly good job but tried to close too soon, and the customers felt rushed and a bit panicky. Mistakes like this show you where you need to work a little harder. You may even lose the sale. But at least you tried to close.

Although you hate to have an unsuccessful close, you have to understand that you're going to experience failure right along with your successes. I'd like you to keep in mind, though, that the real failure is not asking for the business and never asking those closing questions. The failure is when you don't try.

I'm always amazed when I hear salespeople talk about their fears of appearing too pushy or overbearing. I'd say that today's salesperson is just the opposite. Today's salespeople will "relationship" you to death. They spend hours planning and presenting and then leave the customers high and dry wondering how to own the product. We've come to the opposite end of the pendulum, and it's time we find balance in selling. Not too pushy — not too laid back. Build a relationship, but build a successful close in the process.

Adopt a Positive Closing Attitude

Professional salespeople don't step into a selling situation and dread the moment of closing. In fact, they purposefully move toward the close, excited about helping their customers to own. Can you see the difference in attitude between the top producers and those who struggle through each sale? Having a positive attitude toward closing is the key. Also, professionals aren't focused on their gains but instead concentrate on what they can offer the customer — which is why top professionals look forward to a successful close. They know that successfully closing the customer is the only way they'll be able to help the customers find solutions to their problems, discover the riches of owning the product or service, and benefit from the entire process. Because most customers aren't going to ask you to close them, you have to take the initiative. To put yourself in a positive frame of mind, think of closing the sale like this:

✔ Wouldn't you say that your customers deserve to own your product?

✔ Wouldn't you agree that most of them deserve to be served by an honest, hardworking salesperson such as yourself?

✔ Aren't you slighting your customer — depriving them of the opportunity to own your product — by not providing them that opportunity?

I can honestly tell you that when you go into a selling situation with this attitude about closing, you're going to be better prepared to ask for the business and close the transaction. As you change your attitude, your customers will do the same — and everybody wins.

Every closing has one thing in common — success! Create success in your future selling situations by becoming a competent closer. Look at closing as a means to a happy end, not an end to a selling situation. Think of closing as an opening: Opening the doors to a future in sales that promises you and your customers endless opportunity.

Chapter 2
The Anatomy of a Close

· ·

· ·

*A*natomy is the study of separating parts in order to ascertain their relation to each other — that's Merriam Webster's definition, anyway, with a bit of my own interpretation added. Although I don't cover traditional anatomy in this chapter, I do dissect the "anatomy" of a close — and in the process, answer the questions that I'm most often asked about closing:

✔ When do I close?

✔ Where is the best place to close?

✔ How do I close?

There is a bit of psychology behind the answers to each of these questions. In this chapter, I tell you what has worked best in my own personal selling experiences and in the experiences of my students over the years.

When I talk about closing the sale, I assume that up to the final close, you've done everything else right — your potential clients like you, trust you, and feel good in your presence; you've discovered your clients' needs; and you've demonstrated to them that you have just the right product or service to meet those needs. In other words, you're prepared to get the final agreement.

When you make the decision to ask the closing question, you do so based on the information and feedback your client has provided you, the buying signs you've noticed, the body language you've observed, and so on.

In this chapter, I dissect closing in four sections: when to close, where to close, how to try a test close, and skillfully moving into the final close. Taking a serious look at the final closing moments entails dissecting the close into these various sections, understanding each section, and figuring out how they work together so that you can master the overall closing process. That's why I titled this chapter "The Anatomy of a Close." So, grab your scalpel and get to work!

Recognizing When to Close

At my seminars, students ask me *"When* do I close?" The answer is this: Watch your potential clients for a few signs. Clients display some telltale clues when they want the benefits of your product or service. I call these clues buying signs.

A *buying sign* is an indication from your potential clients that lets you know they're prepared to go further. Always be on the lookout for two types of buying signs: verbal and visual.

Verbal buying signs

Verbal buying signs let you know that your clients are interested in owning your product or service — they start when your clients make positive comments about your product or service, ask pointed questions, ask you to repeat something, or speed up the buying pace.

One particular question — the technical question — lets you know that they're interested in owning the product. A *technical question* is any question that your clients don't need to know the answer to unless they own the product. You should pay particular attention to the following types of questions:

- ✔ If you sell computer equipment, your clients may ask, "How much RAM does this computer come with?"

- ✔ A technical question about a copier may be "How will it handle runs of 500 copies?" or "How long does the toner last?"

- ✔ Potential home buyers may ask, "How much are the property taxes?" or "What does the electric bill run each month?"

- ✔ A technical question about a new vehicle may be "What type of gas mileage can I expect to get?" or "What type of warranty does the car come with?"

Few people ask these technical questions unless they're seriously thinking about owning the product or service — a clue that it may be time to close.

Another verbal buying sign occurs when clients ask you to repeat some information. Whenever a buyer says, "Could you go over that again?" I want you to say, "Hot dog! Clients never ask me to repeat information unless they're serious about going ahead." With this type of verbal buying sign, the clients are slowing down the buying pace a bit, but they're still giving you an indication that they're getting ready to close.

Some clients, on the other hand, may speed up the buying pace — and clue you in with verbal buying signs — when they're ready to close. These clients take it slow when doing their research, but as soon as they make a decision, they're ready to get the details behind them and move on to their next project. In this type of case, the clients may give you a synopsis of all the benefits, conduct a quick review of the financial aspects, ask if their interpretation of the information is correct, and look for a pen to approve the paperwork — or reach for their wallets.

Recognizing verbal buying signs is often a matter of listening well — but how do you know if you listen well or not? Here's a test: At any given moment with a customer, you should be able to do the following:

✔ Clarify your customer's needs.

✔ Offer feedback on the areas the customer questions, is unclear on, or is not yet educated in regarding the product or service.

✔ Reinforce the benefits of your product or service that are specific to the customer's needs.

I talk at length about turning features into benefits in *Sales Prospecting For Dummies.*

✔ Evaluate the depth of your customer's commitment to making a decision today.

You do this with test or trial closes that I talk about in this chapter.

✔ Assess the customer's ability to own — does your customer have the money?

This is part of the qualification step of the selling cycle, done mainly by asking questions.

(See Chapter 5 for all of the details on questioning and offering feedback.)

When you've listened this well while conversing with your customers, you know that you're tuned in to their verbal buying signs.

Visual buying signs

Visual buying signs are more subtle than verbal signs and involve an understanding of *body language* — the visual cues we all give to others, consciously or unconsciously, by our posture, facial expressions, and hand gestures. Body language plays a tremendous role in any communication process. The nonverbal communications in Table 2-1 are just a few of the ones I've recognized over the last 20 years.

Table 2-1	Interpreting Body Language
Body Language	**Interpretation**
Crossing arms in front of chest	Not open to new ideas, not listening
Tapping pen, fingers, or shoes	Bored, aggravated, impatient
Leaning back in chair; pressing fingers together	Confident, in control
Taking glasses off; putting stem in mouth	Interested, but needs a slower pace
Looking at watch or clock	You've gone on too long
Wrinkled brow, opened mouth	You've just delivered a surprise

Here are a few other visual buying signs that indicate a customer is ready to close:

- ✔ Clients leaning closer to you
- ✔ Previously nervous or unfriendly customer warming up to you
- ✔ Buyers starting to smile
- ✔ Clients intently reading some paperwork you've given them
- ✔ Clients viewing the product again
- ✔ Clients touching the product again, rereading a brochure, tasting another sample, and so on

Observing your clients . . .

Visually observing your prospective clients means looking at everything that surrounds them as well as the signals they give you. For example, if you get a chance to see a client's office, take a look at the office furniture, wall decorations, desk pictures, and organizational habits. Look at the predominant colors of the office, the seating arrangement, and the place your customer decides to position himself or herself. If you meet on neutral ground and it's your customer's choice, pay attention to the chosen meeting place — it may be his or her favorite restaurant or favorite hotel lobby. Or you may even meet at the client's home. Everything you see at the meeting place should add to the overall impression you develop about your client.

As an expert closer, you can turn these observations into an opportunity to close. Here's an example:

I can tell by the fine quality of furnishings in your office that you are a person who is concerned about giving the proper impression about your business. We at XYZ Cleaning understand how it can hurt that impression if your offices are not kept "white glove" clean. In our Service Excellence Decree, which each member of our staff commits to, we promise that if at any time you're not satisfied, one phone call will bring us — the person responsible to meet your cleaning needs, his or her direct supervisor, and me — here within the hour to correct anything you may be dissatisfied with. This is the quality of service that you and your company deserve, isn't it?

. . . while they observe you!

While you're visually observing your clients, keep in mind that they'll be observing you, too. You always want to look your best and be on your best behavior. Determine the judgments you want your clients to make when they meet you by controlling the image you convey through your appearance and business demeanor.

Make sure you practice the following closing techniques so that you close with confidence:

✔ Use everyday language

✔ Use comfortable mannerisms

✔ Stand or sit with a dignified posture

✔ Convey complete competence

You want your future clients to be sure that you're able to provide your service or deliver your product better than your competitors.

You may encounter a wide variety of buying signs over the course of your career. Some clients may be ready to close after they give one buying sign. Other clients may have to give you five or six buying signs before they're ready to close. Nothing beats personal experience. The more situations you have to learn from, the better you can be at judging when the time is right. Until then, if you see a couple of buying signs, ask a test closing question such as:

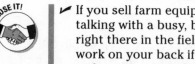

How do you feel so far about everything we've discussed?

If the customer gushes that everything's wonderful, go for the close. If she shows any hesitation, keep talking about her needs and the benefits that your product provides.

Choosing Where to Close

The quick answer to "Where should I close?" is "Anywhere!" You close wherever the client is standing or sitting when you recognize his or her buying signs.

- ✔ If you sell farm equipment and you're in the middle of a field talking with a busy, but interested, farmer, you should close right there in the field! Let the farmer authorize the paperwork on your back if you have to. Mastering that ability can make you outstanding in your field. (Pun intended!)

- ✔ If you sell health products and you're in the locker room of a gym when someone shows interest, close right there in your underwear if you must. That's the fun thing about closing — you can do it anywhere.

- ✔ If you represent a cleaning service or security system for which you need to walk through an entire home, you should carry a clipboard or notepad with your paperwork readily available so that you can close in the hallway if you have to.

- ✔ If you have a pool cleaning service or landscaping service, be prepared to close in the yard or on the patio or the hood of your truck if need be.

- ✔ In a retail setting, closing may occur in the aisle or in a fitting room as well as at the cash register.

Finding a neutral location

When deciding where to close, your best bet is to find a *neutral location* — not on your turf or your client's.

Using a closing room

In some businesses, the company wants you to move from a showroom floor to an area called a *closing room* by your colleagues in the business. This room is usually just a little bit larger than a walk-in closet and contains either a small desk or table and some so-so chairs. It may or may not have a phone, artwork or posters on the wall, or a window — the decor definitely wouldn't win Martha Stewart's approval. But that's okay, because the closing room's sole purpose is for reviewing details and getting a final agreement.

Never, never, never refer to that location as a closing room within earshot of anyone who could ever possibly be a customer! The term "closing room" creates fear, destroys the rapport you've built to this point, and probably even raises the hairs on the backs of your customers' necks — not a good thing when your goal is to set your customer at ease. (See Chapter 6 for more on words and phrases to avoid.)

If your company requires that you take your customers to a closing room, take it in stride and learn to guide your potential clients to the room smoothly, perhaps offering them a soda or glass of water or suggesting a place for them to relax while you serve their needs.

Mastering the Test Close

A *test close* is a question you ask to get a reading on how the client feels (so far) about everything you've been discussing. A test close helps you draw out and overcome objections, create urgency, and obtain clues about your customer's desire to actually close the sale. Think about going to the beach for a moment. What do you do when you get near the water's edge. Do you just run full tilt and jump right in, or do you first get your feet wet to test the temperature of the water? Most people will check the temperature first — that's how I want you to envision a test close. You're getting your feet wet, but are still close enough to shore to be safe. The test close leads you toward closing, but if the response from the client is negative, you haven't caused any discomfort by attempting to close.

A great test close is this:

How are you two feeling so far about the financial program we've been discussing?

If the customers agree that it sounds great, go for the close. If they hesitate, draw them out about the concerns they may have. If they give you a specific concern or objection, handle it. Then, test again with:

> **Are there any other concerns you may have that would keep you from owning this product tonight?**

Test closes are softer and gentler than just asking for the sale. A pro never bluntly asks the buyer to buy the product. You'd never hear a professional salesperson say, "Okay, you want to buy this thing or not?" No, no, no, that's too blunt. Instead, the pros use a test close.

Addressing concerns

I call this phase of the sales process *addressing concerns*. Some people know it as *handling objections*. Either term applies. I teach my students to use the first term, however, because it presents more of an attitude of helpfulness rather than overcoming a challenge. Refer to Chapter 6 for other terms that help present you in a better light.

Average salespeople tend to cringe internally upon hearing a customer express a concern about their product or service. The pros, however, get excited. If they object, they're interested. Think about it. Would you waste your time objecting to something that you have no interest in owning?

Champion salespeople sometimes flush out objections with test closes — questions that determine how ready people are to make buying decisions, covered in the previous section — recognizing that they need to uncover some unidentified objections. Usually, concerns are about money, but in some cases, concerns will be the time frame or time required to change over to the wonderful new gizmo that you're selling.

The initial way that customers express concern is that they can't commit to a product or service. When your clients say they're "not sure" about a product, you know that it's time to fish for the details they aren't sure about and answer their questions. Be sincerely concerned and ask your customers to help you understand by trying the following:

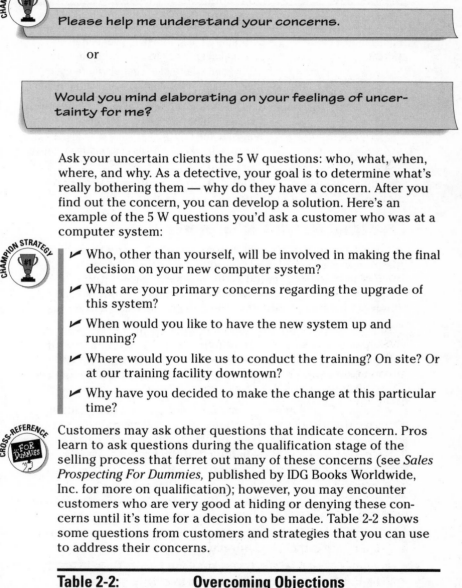

CHAMPION STRATEGY #1

Please help me understand your concerns.

or

Would you mind elaborating on your feelings of uncertainty for me?

Ask your uncertain clients the 5 W questions: who, what, when, where, and why. As a detective, your goal is to determine what's really bothering them — why do they have a concern. After you find out the concern, you can develop a solution. Here's an example of the 5 W questions you'd ask a customer who was at a computer system:

CHAMPION STRATEGY #1

✔ Who, other than yourself, will be involved in making the final decision on your new computer system?

✔ What are your primary concerns regarding the upgrade of this system?

✔ When would you like to have the new system up and running?

✔ Where would you like us to conduct the training? On site? Or at our training facility downtown?

✔ Why have you decided to make the change at this particular time?

CROSS-REFERENCE FOR DUMMIES

Customers may ask other questions that indicate concern. Pros learn to ask questions during the qualification stage of the selling process that ferret out many of these concerns (see *Sales Prospecting For Dummies,* published by IDG Books Worldwide, Inc. for more on qualification); however, you may encounter customers who are very good at hiding or denying these concerns until it's time for a decision to be made. Table 2-2 shows some questions from customers and strategies that you can use to address their concerns.

Table 2-2: Overcoming Objections

Client Says . . .	You Need To . . .
"Well, we need more time to decide."	Take a look at the overcoming-procrastination closes in Chapter 7.

(continued)

Table 2-2: *(continued)*

Client Says . . .	You Need To . . .
"I don't think I can afford it."	Be prepared to increase the value the potential client sees in the product or service to the point where she'll benefit more by having the product than by keeping her money.
"It won't fit in our garage."	Help them discover other places to put the new speedboat, such as a covered area alongside the house, their very own slip at the marina, a storage yard, or at a relative's house.

For additional ways to address customer's concerns, check out my book, *Selling For Dummies* (IDG Books Worldwide, Inc.).

Creating a state of urgency

Sometimes clients think that they're not at all ready to own at this time, but as soon as you establish an urgency, they feel the sense of urgency, too, and decide they really do want the product. The next thing you know — they own it! The following list shows some examples of how you can create a sense of urgency:

✔ If you sell real estate, create urgency by letting your buyer know that the seller is highly motivated and will likely take the first offer that's presented — or let her know that interest rates may rise and change the amount of house she can afford.

✔ If a product is in great demand, the potential of dwindling inventory could spur someone on to making a decision to own the latest color laser printer today, rather than delaying the decision and then finding that the product is back-ordered with no definite delivery date.

✔ If you sell financial services, remind clients that the sooner they begin investing, the sooner their money starts earning more money! Create urgency by showing charts on how much more clients will need to put aside each month at a later date rather than how little they need to start now.

✔ If you own a boat dealership, remind clients that boats are in high demand just before the Fourth of July, so a June purchase is wise.

✔ As a contractor, help clients see the logic in remodeling in time for a major holiday, such as Thanksgiving or Christmas.

Suggesting to customers that they place their orders today in order to guarantee their needs are met in a timely manner, creates urgency and knocks some customers off the "indecision fence."

Moving into the Final Close

A final close happens when you decide to ask the buyer to make a decision. The moment is right when you believe that you've presented the product or service in a manner that demonstrates that it meets the customer's needs, have answered all of her questions, and have covered the financial aspects of the transaction. After you ask the final closing question, you wrap up the sale in one of two ways: with a signature on your paperwork or with an exchange of money.

Shifting to paperwork

Suppose your business requires you to fill out paperwork as the final stage in a close. The close begins by moving to the paperwork after your test close receives a favorable response. How, though, do you move to your paperwork without an obvious shifting of gears?

The least obvious way to shift to paperwork is to have paperwork in front of your clients *during the sales process.* Get permission from your clients to take notes early in the sale, which gets them comfortable with the paperwork. Chapter 4 has a bunch more information for you, but here's a script that you can use early in your presentation:

> I want to do the best job I can for you today. So would you be offended if, while we chat, I make a few notes? That way I won't possibly forget anything we discuss that could save you time or money.

If you haven't taken notes throughout the sale, though, you can still move to paperwork in a variety of ways.

The "Let me make a note of that" approach

Suppose that, in response to your test close, your clients ask how soon they can receive a product. (This is called a porcupine question, which is covered in Chapter 5.) Here's a script to try:

Them:	How soon can we get the product?
You:	How soon would you like to begin enjoying this product?
Them:	We're having guests over on the holiday weekend. I'd sure like to have it by then.
You:	Let me make a note of that.

And you're into your paperwork.

The "Let's draft up our feelings" approach

Some people may react negatively if you say you're going to "put the whole thing together" and then let them take a look at it. You may be moving too fast for some clients; they may think you're being pushy. You're better off to calmly and sincerely ask a test question to determine where they are in the decision process. If the response is positive, then move — again gently — to your paperwork.

> How are you feeling about all of this so far?

or

You:	Do you see why we're so excited about this product [service]?
Them:	It sounds great.
You:	Well, then let's just draft up our feelings about the product on paper to see if it even makes sense.

What an excellent way to move on to your paperwork.

The "You can take the facts with you" approach

Clients who are a little nervous during your presentation may become even more nervous when you turn to paperwork. Here's a way to help them relax:

> **You:** Well, then let's just draft up the paperwork to see if it even makes sense.
>
> **Them:** Okay, but would you leave those papers with us so we could look at them?
>
> **You:** I'll do anything you want me to do, but let's just get down all the facts so you'll really have something to consider.

If you sense hesitation from your clients, that's okay. Simply exude confidence that after all the information is on paper, it'll make more sense to them. You may also want to reinforce that your paperwork doesn't entail any kind of commitment to buy at this time.

The "Let's outline the details" approach

When you begin any paperwork, your clients may start getting cold feet and may stop you. This type of reaction is normal. Expect it. Plan for it. Here's a way to handle it:

> **Them:** Wait, we're not sure about this.
>
> **You:** I understand how you feel. I'm only outlining the details of the transaction so we can carefully analyze the best course of action to take.

Be sure to warmly relieve the customer's fears by smiling as you begin the paperwork.

The "correct spelling" or "middle initial" approach

Another way to begin paperwork is called the *order blank close,* when you ask a test close question such as the following:

> What is the correct spelling of your last name?

Only use this technique, of course, if your client has an unusual name; don't try this approach if the client's last name is Jones or Brown.

Another order blank close is as follows:

> **What is your correct mailing address here?**

When working with two people, one of my favorite ways to use the order blank close is to analyze which of the two people is the most favorable about going ahead. Then just smile, look that person in the eyes, and ask for his or her middle initial.

Is the client going to have to think about that one? Oh, sure, I can hear the client now, "Well, I used to have a middle initial. I just haven't used it in ages. Now, let me think. . . ." If this situation does happen to you, you're not talking with a competent, qualified decision maker.

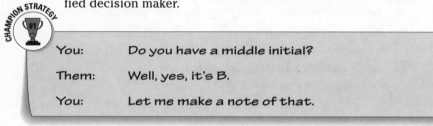

You:	Do you have a middle initial?
Them:	Well, yes, it's B.
You:	Let me make a note of that.

You're on your way to the paperwork.

The "Do you know the date?" approach

Ask any cashier in the grocery store and he or she'll probably tell you that at least one in ten customers ask for the date as they begin writing their checks. This statistic shouldn't come as a surprise, though — we're all busy people and keeping the calendar fresh in our minds isn't always one of life's major details. In some fields of sales, you may give four presentations, field a dozen calls, talk to eight prospective buyers, and put out three fires before noon!

This craziness presents another method for moving on to your paperwork — simply verify the date with your clients. You won't look incompetent; if you've acted professionally and sincerely up to that point, your clients won't give this question a second thought. They'll answer it by reflex. In fact, they may have to glance at a wall calendar or their watch to verify it for themselves, unless today's date has special meaning to them (besides being the day they invest in your product!).

> **You:** You know, I've been running at such a pace that I've lost track of time. Do you know the date?
>
> **Them:** It's May 23rd.
>
> **You:** Let me make a note of that.

or (to make it a bit humorous)

> **You:** Let's see, today's date is the twelfth already, isn't it?
>
> **Them:** Yes, Tom it is.
>
> **You:** Wow. Time is sure flying. Let me get that down before it's tomorrow already.

And then, chuckle just a bit. Chances are they'll chuckle with you and not object to seeing you begin writing your paperwork.

The "I'll need your approval" approach

This approach is the most uncomplicated way of getting to a final agreement. You may have customers who are willing to go ahead — there's been little hesitation and few objections. Everyone in the room agrees that it's in their best interests to invest in your product.

At this point, don't fuss or get fancy. Simply put all the details down on paper. Review those details for accuracy, and then turn the paper around in front of your clients. As you hand over a pen, say the following:

> In analyzing all considerations, I sincerely feel this decision makes good sense. With your approval right here, we'll arrange delivery and begin giving you the finest service possible.

or

I'll just need your approval to set up everything.

After that conversation, just point to the line, put your pen on top of your paperwork, sit back, and let your clients make the decision. This may seem a bit simplified, but simplicity is a good thing when you're asking someone to make a decision. We cover this strategy in greater detail in Chapter 4.

Closing the retail sale

When you work in a retail setting such as a clothing store, most customers simply bring their purchases to a cash register when they're ready to close. However, as a retail salesperson, you need to walk the floor of the store, tend to the fitting rooms, move about the aisles helping customers find what they want, and make suggestions — rather than simply standing behind a cash register, waiting for customers.

In retail sales, the entire selling cycle may take less than ten minutes, which is not very long for you to sell *and* close the sale.

Know your paperwork

While you fill out your paperwork, you must always chitchat with your clients. You can't remain silent. In order to keep talking, though, you must know your paperwork by rote.

When I was a sales manager, all of my new salespeople were required to complete at least ten copies of our paperwork before their first sales call. They had to know where the date needed to go, what order of the

details were necessary to complete a transaction, and they had to rehearse turning the paperwork around to the customer for approval.

My heart goes out to salespeople who lose sales because the paperwork is foreign to them. Any piece of paper you fill out must be as familiar as your best friend — you should memorize it before you ever begin a sales call.

The "Let me reserve a fitting room for you" approach

In retail sales, placing an item in your customer's hands is the only way to close a sale. Physical involvement creates emotional involvement — and people buy emotionally. You have a variety of options to get your product into (or onto) your customers' laps, mouths, backs, feet, and so on!

- ✔ Grocery stores offer free samples.

- ✔ Upscale cosmetics companies offer personal makeovers.

- ✔ Athletic shoe stores let you walk or run around the store before you buy.

- ✔ Car dealers promote test drives.

- ✔ Furniture stores let you try an item in your home before you buy.

- ✔ Home improvement stores showcase expensive cabinets in kitchen-like settings.

- ✔ Magazines offer free trial subscriptions.

The bottom line is that customers need to physically touch your product. Here's an example:

> **Them:** Well, I kind of like this color. I'm not sure about the style.
>
> **You:** The best way to determine if you're comfortable with any style is to try it on. Let me reserve one of our fitting rooms for you. I'll hang this dress up on the outside of the door so that you'll know which dressing room is yours.

The "Will this be cash, check, or charge" approach

As soon as a customer indicates a desire to own your product, take the product from her. Here's an example:

> **Them:** I like this outfit.
>
> **You:** This is a good color for your skin tone. I'll be happy to take this up to the register for you. Will this be cash, check, or charge?

If you have the product in your hands that the customers have indicated they want and you start to walk away, the clients are going to follow you or stop you to possibly add on to their purchase. Either way, you're winning.

Chapter 3

The Anatomy of a Closer

In This Chapter

▶ Becoming a champion closer

▶ Recognizing a top closer

▶ Improving your own closing traits

*I*n order to become a top closer, you need to know how a closer acts, what he or she looks like, and a bit about a great closer's attitudes, systems and styles. In this chapter, I show you what a top closer looks like so you can see how you measure up. Hopefully, you're a pretty close match and the rest of this book will prepare you to stretch to that top professional level. Even if you do find some discrepancies, that's okay. You're heading in the right direction by reading on.

In *Selling For Dummies,* I cover the ten steps to professionalism in sales, which is a good starting point for anyone wanting to achieve success in this wonderful profession. In this chapter, I talk specifically about people whose aim is to achieve true champion status in their field of selling. Top producers obtain champion status by closing more sales than anyone else in the company. They earn the highest incomes. They win the exotic trips that are awarded as prizes for contests. They drive the nicest cars. They may even seem to have the nicest clients. (That last one isn't necessarily true; rather, it's probably just a reflection of that old adage, "people give what they get." In other words, the clients are treated well by this top closer, which is why the clients are nice in return.)

Finding the Champion Closer in You

Could you recognize a champion closer if you saw one walking down the street? Are you able to pick the great closers out of a crowd? Chances are good that you can't. When you're a client talking to a champion closer, you may not even realize it until sometime after the sale when you start analyzing just why it was that you actually enjoyed yourself during the selling process. But there is one thing you should be able to recognize: whether or not a great closer is staring back at you from your mirror every morning.

If there's any doubt in your mind right now, take a moment and walk over to a mirror. Look yourself straight in the eye and say these words: "I am a top closing professional." Did your eyes waiver, even just a smidge? If they did, you don't believe that you are a top closing professional at this moment. You have to close yourself first on your desire to become a top closer before you can ever succeed. Say it again, with gusto: "I am a top closing professional." Repeat it over and over again every time you are in front of a mirror for the next 21 days, and you'll begin to believe it. Better yet, you'll find yourself rather effortlessly making great strides in achieving that "top closer" ranking in your company.

So how do you become a top closer? Here's some steps you can follow to become the best:

1. **Recognize particular traits and skills of champion closers.**

   I list several of those traits in the "Anatomical Features of a Top Closer" section of this chapter.

2. **Determine how many of those traits and skills you already have.**

   Take the personal inventory test at the end of this chapter.

3. **Make a personal plan for developing or enhancing those skills you may not have at 100 percent competency.**

   For each trait listed in this chapter, I give you a plan for developing that skill.

4. **Work on your personal plan daily!**

   In order to master anything, you have to put forth the effort required to train. When you see Olympic athletes parading into the arena at the opening ceremony of the game, they all look like winners, don't they? And they are. They've already beat hundreds or thousands of other athletes to make the team — and the athletes who didn't make the cut are sitting at home, probably because they didn't train quite enough. Even an hour more or less per week can make a difference between being in the top 5 percent or not.

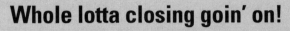

Whole lotta closing goin' on!

Closing the sale begins with your initial contact with prospective clients.

✔ You are closing the prospects on being open to you and your ideas.

✔ You close them on arranging a time to meet.

✔ You close them on being willing to give you answers to your questions.

✔ You close them on your product or service during your presentation.

✔ You close them on your answers to their concerns.

✔ You close them on authorizing the paperwork that will bring them the benefits of your product or service and bring you additional income.

Anatomical Features of a Top Closer

The first step to becoming a top closer is figuring out how to recognize a top closer and everything the top closer uses to be the best. To help illustrate this point, I take parts of the human anatomy and show how each part is vital in achieving champion status. The following sections cover each part in more detail, but here's a quick summary:

✔ A brain that fully comprehends all that it sees.

✔ A heart that can lead.

✔ Eyes that read the written word.

✔ Ears that listen twice as much as the mouth speaks.

✔ Strong shoulders that carry burdens — their own and those of their clients.

✔ Stomach enough to face challenges on an hourly basis.

✔ Legs willing to stand up for what they believe in: their product or service and how it will satisfy the needs of the client.

✔ Feet willing to walk the extra mile for anyone.

Is this the anatomy you see reflected in your mirror? If not, I strongly recommend that you tape this list up on your mirror and review it regularly. Put a copy of it in your daily planner, too.

Repetition is the mother of learning. Reminding yourself of these traits and striving to achieve them will soon become second nature.

Preparation is key

Because so much closing goes on in everyday selling situations, you're wise to prepare yourself as well as you possibly can. Not knowing when a closing opportunity may arise, you need to be prepared not just between 9 a.m. and 5 p.m., Monday through Friday: You must be prepared every waking moment to sniff out opportunities and react properly to those you find.

✔ Remember to take care of yourself. You've probably seen co-workers or clients at one time or another who were overly tired. You could tell just by the way they walked that they weren't at 100 percent that day. Well, surprise, surprise — your clients will notice this in you as well. A lack of sleep will have a detrimental effect on your ability to be enthusiastic and to pay attention to details. In other words, achieving champion status in your selling career will be tough if you don't take care of yourself.

✔ Schedule time for planning time. Know what you can and cannot realistically accomplish based on your current commitments before making new commitments to clients.

✔ Read, reread, practice out loud, and drill yourself on recognizing verbal and visual buying signs. Master the appropriate response for each, as I cover in Chapter 2.

✔ Develop, and then commit to memory, at least four test closes for each product or service you represent. Test closes are used to determine how ready the client is to go ahead with making a buying decision. Flip to Chapter 2 for a review of this strategy.

✔ Master the six steps to overcoming objections, so that you can move on to closing the sale. I cover those steps in great detail in Chapter 11 of *Selling For Dummies* (IDG Books Worldwide, Inc.).

✔ Know your product inside and out. Read everything on the product. Use it yourself. Get feedback from happy clients. Know the current inventory situation, too.

In order to become a top champion closer, memorize these words: "I will do unto others as they wish to be done to." Then, put these words into every act of service you perform. (This phrase is a professional, service-oriented version of the Golden Rule.) Practice this new approach with your family and friends, and you'll quickly realize the benefits of this new way of relating to others. After it becomes a habit, you'll find that your clients are becoming the nicest clients around.

A closer's brain: Always alert

In order for your brain to best comprehend what your eyes and ears are capturing, you must have the ability to be focused in the present moment. Such focus involves developing your powers of concentration. Being able to focus your concentration means leaving everything unrelated to the present moment outside the door when you meet with your client. If you do most of your closing in a remote manner, as I cover in Chapter 9, develop a simple strategy to clear your mind before making the connection with a client. Some of my students mentally "flush" their previous thoughts with picture images of water rushing over them and washing them away. Find what works for you and then use it.

To empower your brain, make these promises to yourself:

✔ I will take courses on meditation to improve concentration.

✔ I will keep up with my company's product information.

✔ I will read industry news.

Fulfilling these three promises will get you started on building your brain power. What will probably happen next is that you become extremely curious about everything and anything that could have a positive impact on your career, whether it's selling skills, product knowledge, industry news, advancements in technology, or better ways of learning.

A closer's heart: Leading by example

No one wants to do business with the salesperson who's at the bottom of the pack with your company. Everyone wants to work with a winner! Winners not only outshine others with their selling skills, but acquire leadership skills as well. A top closer needs to have leadership skills. Regardless of what you're doing in life, you're either leading or following at all times. As a parent, you lead your children. As a spouse, there are times when you take the lead and other times when you follow. As an employer, you lead your people. As an employee, you choose to follow the lead of the decision makers at your company. As a closer, you attempt to lead your prospects to the best solution for their needs, which is your product or service.

Learning from the greats

During the past two years, a highlight of my life has been to share the seminar stage with some of the greatest leaders in current history. Through my association with the Peter Lowe International "Success" seminars, I've had the opportunity to meet and talk with many people including retired General Colin Powell, former First Lady Barbara Bush, retired General Norman Schwartzkopf, motivational legend and dear friend, Zig Ziglar, and Peter Lowe, who has developed an exceptional day-long seminar featuring expert speakers who enhance the lives of the hundreds of thousands of students they reach. I've tried hard to assume the role of student and learn as much as possible from our times together. The most powerful lessons I've learned have been about leadership and how those skills apply daily to not only business situations, but to our personal lives as well.

✔ For example, General Schwartzkopf has a great definition of a leader that he shared with me. He said, "A great leader is an average individual who is extremely well prepared when an incredible event occurs."

If you think about General Schwartzkopf's definition, it tells us that anyone can become a great leader. After all, we're all pretty much average at the moment of birth, right? As babies, we have the same basic mentality and skill levels. What we do as we grow to prepare ourselves for life's great challenges is what makes the difference in our leadership abilities.

✔ Renowned motivational speaker Zig Ziglar has a similar definition: "Effective leaders develop the ability to see things from the other person's perspective. They sell the advantages of cooperation rather than demanding it."

A professional in the field of selling never comes across in a demanding manner — that would be demeaning to the client. Good closers are good at selling not only products and services, but also the benefits of working with their company and themselves.

If you want to be considered a great leader at some time in your life, you need to be well prepared. What is the essence of leadership?

✔ The ability to make your followers believe that you possess superior knowledge of the situation, greater wisdom to cope with the unknown, and greater moral force — belief that you will do the right thing.

✔ Experience in a wide range of situations and the ability to assess the current situation quickly and apply the previously learned knowledge when appropriate.

To improve your leadership qualities, try the following:

✔ Take in every new experience with the attitude of a student. Look for ways to apply these new experiences to leadership situations.

✔ Seek out opportunities to lead so you can develop your skills. Become a volunteer both in your personal and business situations.

✔ Watch other leaders carefully to understand how they communicate their wishes to their followers.

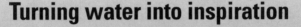

Turning water into inspiration

Greater wisdom comes from study that's tested by experience. One of the best examples is an incident in the life of Alexander the Great.

Three hundred years before Christ, Alexander the Great led a forced march across a hot and desolate plain. On the eleventh day, he and all the soldiers who were still with him were near death from thirst. Still Alexander pressed on. At midday, two scouts brought him what little water they had been able to find — it barely filled the bottom of a helmet. Their throats burning, Alexander's men stood back and watched him enviously, knowing that as the leader, he deserved the first drink of water. Alexander didn't hesitate. He turned the helmet over and poured the water on the hot sand at his feet. Then he said, "It's of no use for one to drink when many thirst." The men desperately needed water — large quantities of it — but Alexander had only a few drops. So he gave them the only thing he did have: inspiration to keep moving forward.

That's leadership.

ANECDOTE

A book can be your best friend

Early in my career, my wife and I were invited to the home — a mansion, actually — of a very wealthy man who was one of my clients. As he took us on a tour of his beautiful home, I noticed his eyes light up with extra pride as we entered the room he valued the most. This special room wasn't his home theater or the room where he entertained. The room was his library. Having the walls lined with great books — most of which he had already read — was a great source of joy to him. The books served as a visual reminder of his dedication to continuing his education. He knew that if he didn't continually strive to learn more, he would stop achieving the income he was earning and could stand to lose the assets he had accumulated thus far.

Dedicate yourself to becoming an avid reader. This dedication will reap dividends beyond your wildest dreams!

A closer's eyes: Reading into every situation

Nearly all professionals pride themselves on being avid readers. One man I know has committed to reading at least one book per week. (And he doesn't mean the latest Stephen King novel.) He reads biographies of great people. He reads books on management. He reads financial information that is pertinent to his particular field of endeavor, and yes, he does occasionally read a good novel. This man wasn't always an avid reader. He learned, like I did, that top professionals value their ability to learn more than any other skill, and one of the easiest and most effective ways to learn anything is to read. He set reading goals for himself and then followed through. By continually pushing himself, he has gotten better and faster at reading, therefore learning more all the time.

To improve your reading skills, make the following promises to yourself:

- ✔ I will read something related to my career daily.
- ✔ I will start (or maintain) my own personal development library.
- ✔ I commit to reading one book every ____ days. (You fill in the blank.)

ANECDOTE

You need the speed

For anyone who has a large volume of reading to keep up with (someone like a champion closer), doubling your reading speed while maintaining or improving comprehension levels through a speed reading course may be worth the investment of a whole day at a seminar. Besides, your investment in the course can save you a whole day of reading over a period of just a couple of months. I strongly recommend the Evelyn Wood courses (or any speed reading course) for anyone over the age of 12.

A closer's ears: Hearing clients out

The single best communication skill you can develop is your ability to listen with your ears — I mean truly listen to whoever is doing the talking. Develop the self-discipline to listen more than you talk — let your prospective client do most of the talking. Look at it this way: When you talk, you're giving information you already know. When someone else is talking and you're listening, you're getting new information (hopefully, it's information that will tell you just what the buyer wants to own).

The challenge that most of us have with our listening skills is that we attempt to formulate our next question and comments while the other person is still talking. We do this because we want to come across like we're on the ball. This is a bad habit that average closers have. You, however, want to be a top closer. Top closers listen intently, focusing on the words being spoken as well as the body language. When the client is done talking, top closers let a pause occur while they formulate their next questions and answers. This simple strategy goes a long way toward showing your prospects that you were really listening to them. You show the client that you've taken in what they just told you as new information and are processing it, just for them. You show that your next suggestion or recommendation is going to be customized just for them. This careful listening makes your clients feel important — and that's just how a top closer wants them to feel.

The pause is one of the most powerful tools you can use in presenting and closing. If you are ever in doubt as to whether or not the prospects are paying attention to you, simply pause. If they were drifting, the silence will jerk them back to the present moment — and have them wondering what they missed every time.

Ever notice how people often feel compelled to fill silent moments with talk? The more you remain silent, the more likely the other person is to jump in and start talking. By developing your questioning skills (as Chapter 5 discusses in detail), you'll be able to simply ask the right question or two to get the clients going or to encourage them to continue. Here's an example of how to do this:

> You obviously have a reason for saying that. Would you mind elaborating on your point?

See how simple this is? All you have to do is show that you're interested in knowing more. Believe me, most people are willing to tell all kinds of things to someone with a good ear for listening.

If you're a talker and you don't really listen to what the clients have to say, their interest in what you have to say will lessen. If you show interest in your clients and what they have to say, you encourage them to talk. I stress this point when teaching to my students.

To become a champion closer, you must adopt the attitude of an *interested introvert* rather than what a stereotypical salesperson is — an *interesting extrovert*. Be interested in the clients' needs, their situation, their history. You need this information to be able to make a wise recommendation and go for the close.

Here are some strategies for improving your listening skills:

- ✔ Clear your mind of all other clients and any personal challenges when you're with a particular client.
- ✔ Develop the ability to keep quiet and let the client talk.
- ✔ Master the use of the planned pause to keep the client's attention.

A closer's backbone: Shouldering the burden

The strength of your backbone is revealed in the set of your shoulders. Have you ever met someone with a weak backbone — someone who didn't have a strong character and gave up at the least resistance? Would you want to invest in a product being sold by that person? A champion sales closer must have a strong, healthy backbone and become a person with character, determination, and fortitude.

Champion closers always look like they could bear the weight of the world on their shoulders and keep on ticking. Your clients will take comfort in this. They may be having some challenges related to their needs and want someone to talk to about their concerns. Or your clients may just be having a tough day, and your visit could be the highlight of it because when you're there, they know you're there for them, leaving your personal burdens behind. That's a top closer.

To strengthen your shoulders for the job at hand:

✔ Pay close attention to your posture.

✔ Become a person of character.

✔ Don't be afraid to listen and even take on your clients' burdens.

A closer's digestive system: Stomaching the tough times

As a salesperson, especially a top closer, you're bound to encounter tough clients and even tougher situations. How do you handle it when your recommended solution backfires on the client and they've committed to a five-year financing plan? How do you handle an angry client, someone who'd just as soon strangle you as hear from you? A top closer has developed the stomach for these situations. He or she doesn't like facing them any more than anyone else, but they don't try to avoid the tough situations, either. The following conversation shows a tough situation and how the salesperson was able to handle it.

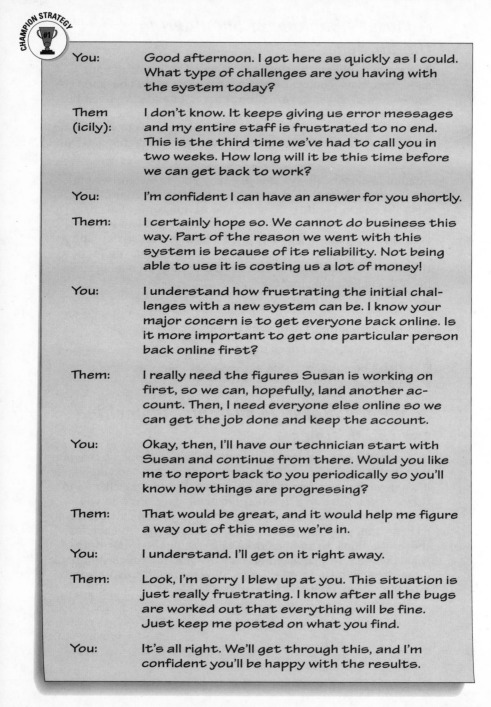

CHAMPION STRATEGY #1

You:	Good afternoon. I got here as quickly as I could. What type of challenges are you having with the system today?
Them (icily):	I don't know. It keeps giving us error messages and my entire staff is frustrated to no end. This is the third time we've had to call you in two weeks. How long will it be this time before we can get back to work?
You:	I'm confident I can have an answer for you shortly.
Them:	I certainly hope so. We cannot do business this way. Part of the reason we went with this system is because of its reliability. Not being able to use it is costing us a lot of money!
You:	I understand how frustrating the initial challenges with a new system can be. I know your major concern is to get everyone back online. Is it more important to get one particular person back online first?
Them:	I really need the figures Susan is working on first, so we can, hopefully, land another account. Then, I need everyone else online so we can get the job done and keep the account.
You:	Okay, then, I'll have our technician start with Susan and continue from there. Would you like me to report back to you periodically so you'll know how things are progressing?
Them:	That would be great, and it would help me figure a way out of this mess we're in.
You:	I understand. I'll get on it right away.
Them:	Look, I'm sorry I blew up at you. This situation is just really frustrating. I know after all the bugs are worked out that everything will be fine. Just keep me posted on what you find.
You:	It's all right. We'll get through this, and I'm confident you'll be happy with the results.

The salesperson has just completed a very successful communication. He not only calmed his client by listening, acknowledging the customer's anger, and asking questions regarding the customer's concerns, but the salesperson defused a potentially explosive situation in which he could have lost not only the client, but his reputation as well.

Review and follow these ten steps to defuse angry clients:

1. **Quickly acknowledge the customer's anger.**

2. **Make it clear to the customer that you are sincerely concerned.**

3. **Don't hurry the customer. Let him vent.**

4. **Stay calm. Take good notes.**

5. **Ask questions.**

6. **Get the customer talking about solutions.**

7. **Agree on a solution.**

8. **Agree on a schedule.**

9. **Keep the customer informed.**

10. **Meet your schedule.**

Top closers carry the weight, take the heat, pick up the slack, do whatever it takes to make the client happy. No matter what the challenge, they know that the faster they get on the problem, the quicker it'll be behind them.

Follow these guidelines to improve how you stomach challenges:

- ✔ Handle any client challenges immediately.

- ✔ Improve detachment skills.

- ✔ Master the ten steps of defusing an angry client.

A closer's legs: Having a leg to stand on

Because of their high level of competency, top closers have a leg to stand on. Top people know the industry better than their peers, which makes them more believable when trying to persuade clients to own their particular product or service. Top closers have the facts and figures to back up what they say. Not only that, top closers take the figures and put them into layman's terms to help the client understand, and therefore trust, the product.

Top closers are ready and willing to put their money where their mouths are. If they're selling a product that's made for general use or consumption, they own it. They use the product they're trying to sell and are able to offer their own personal testimony. If it's insurance or investments they represent, they're ready and willing to use their own personal portfolio to show clients how it all goes together. If they market electronics, they own the latest models and know what all those buttons are for. If the products are vitamins, beauty products, or food items, they consume the products themselves.

If you sell a line of cosmetics and you don't use them yourself, you'll never achieve top ranking in your company. If you sell insurance and don't currently have the maximum coverage recommended for someone in your stage and position in life, you're committing yourself to be average. Potential clients won't believe in what you're selling if you don't.

When you can sell with conviction and enthusiasm for your product or service, you close more sales. Become a product of the product.

To present yourself in your best light with regard to your product or service:

✔ Know more about your product than anyone.

✔ Use the products yourself.

✔ Demonstrate a firm belief in the value of your product.

A closer's feet: Miles to go before I sleep

You've probably heard the saying "To truly understand another person, walk a mile in their shoes." Champion closers do their best to get on the inside of the selling situation:

✔ They put themselves on the same side of the table as the client.

✔ They are experts at perceiving another person's point of view.

✔ They are extremely empathetic.

Every one of these actions demonstrates to the clients that the top closer is willing to walk that mile in their shoes, and then go the extra mile to repair those shoes or show them to a better destination.

CHAMPION STRATEGY #1

Using positive self-talk

Top closers listen to good stuff. I love listening to motivational tapes and upbeat music; they keep me going and help me control the direction of my self-talk. *Self-talk* is that conversation that's running in our heads all the time. There are times when you're aware of it and can work to control it. Other times, you may be preoccupied with the here-and-now and aren't following what's being said subconsciously — that's when self-talk gets dangerous.

Controlling your self-talk is as easy as changing a conversation you're having with another person. Actually, it's easier because you can be rude and interrupt your self-talk when you wouldn't do that to another person. If you hear yourself expressing negative or hurtful thoughts, take control of that conversation and turn that last thought into a hopeful one.

For example, if you get a message that says, "Boy, you never should've mentioned that upgrade coming out in six months. Now the client will probably put off their decision that long. What a dodo!" Take that message and make a conscious effort to tell yourself, "The client really needs help today, so I believe a six-month wait for an upgraded piece of equipment will be too long. They're likely to go ahead with their decision now."

Practice this strategy each time you catch yourself thinking a negative thought or you hear your self-talk taking a turn toward the negative. Being what we are, we are often hardest on ourselves, and our subconscious mind picks up on negative attitudes. However, the subconscious will also pick up on a positive attitude and boost us up if we just pay attention to what we tell it.

Paraphrasing or repeating what clients say shows them once more that you're listening and working hard to truly understand their situation. Making them feel this way is as simple as this:

> From what I'm hearing, it seems your biggest concern is. . . .

or

> Help me understand. Your highest priority on this project appears to be. . . .

If you help them, they will come

If you present an attitude of helpfulness at the beginning of every client contact, you'll become a top closer. By approaching a selling situation with the goal of helping the client, you won't come across aggressively — and by no means will you be average. And with this helpful attitude, there won't be dollar signs in your eyes, which will put the client at ease.

I teach my seminar attendees that a salesperson's income is a scoreboard reflection of the amount of service he or she gives to others. If you're not happy with your current score (income), you need to improve the level of service you are currently offering. Improving your service begins with taking on an attitude of servitude.

It also means taking control of your personal environment — if something's going on in your personal life or in your career that could be taking your attention away from serving others, you may want to set aside some time to deal with it and get past it. Don't risk losing sales or clients because the challenges you face are distracting you from giving them all that they expect and deserve.

Paraphrasing or repeating what clients say is sort of like torpedo radar technology. You're the torpedo and you're attempting to find the right target, which is the proper solution for the client. You send out little signals in the form of questions and suggestions to where you think your target may be. You wait for feedback. If you're too far off course, you readjust your thinking and send out a new signal. Chances are good that you may zigzag through the water many times before you hone in for a direct hit, which is a closed sale.

Top closers are persistent when it comes to striving for that targeted closed sale. They don't give up and turn back to the ship. Imagine what a disaster that would be. Ask anyone in sales who isn't persistent what their professional life is like and you'll see: It's full of disappointment.

As far as walking the extra mile is concerned, always remember this: under-promise and over-deliver. Hey, if you know the food processor you sell not only slices and dices but juices as well, you don't have to tell your customers that right up front (unless they tell you that's what they're looking for). Holding back a tidbit of information or an added benefit can be a very powerful strategy. If the customers have any doubts about going ahead, you can use your tidbit to shove them off the fence of indecisiveness. Holding back that one last product perk can also help conquer buyer's remorse (see Chapter 10 for more information on buyer's remorse): You can use your extra added bonus or feature to keep the sale solid.

To gain mileage with your clients:

✔ Do your best to see things from the client's perspective.

✔ Be persistent in communicating with your clients and providing them with the best service possible.

✔ Wait for and analyze client feedback.

✔ Under-promise and over-deliver.

Diagnosing Your Closing Deficiencies

In looking over the basic anatomy of a top closing champion, how many of the attributes do you think you have pretty well mastered? Hopefully, you've mastered quite a few and this chapter was a good review for you. If you're relatively new to selling and any of the aforementioned anatomy items were a surprise to you, don't let it bother you. Just highlight the ones you feel are most important at this moment. Make a list of those you want to work on right away. Keep it with you and review it several times each day. Be both persistent and patient with yourself. Before long, you'll notice that people sincerely smile when they see you coming. Your customers won't cringe or reach to hide their wallets.

Personal Inventory Test

1. I have an ongoing personal plan for self-improvement.

2. I have mastered questioning skills to the point where I keep the communication moving toward closing the sale.

3. I listen more than I talk.

4. I understand and fluently read body language.

5. I build planning time into my daily schedule.

6. I know at least four test closes for each product that I represent. (See chapter 2 for more on test closes.)

7. I have read everything to date that my company has published on my product or service at least twice.

8. I have talked with satisfied clients for feedback on the products.

9. I am present to those who require my attention.

10. I have my next self-improvement course scheduled.

11. I subscribe to industry news.

12. I seek out competent leaders to learn from.

13. I volunteer for leadership opportunities in order to gain experience.

14. I know how to defuse angry client situations.

15. I have used my own products.

16. I put myself in the client's shoes before attempting to close the sale.

17. I have adopted an attitude of servitude with my clients.

18. I under-promise and over-deliver every time!

Part II
Tactics and Strategies of Champion Closers

"They've been that way for over 10 minutes. Larry's either having a staring contest with the customer, or he's afraid to ask for the sale again."

In this part . . .

This part is where you find the word-for-word closes that have been proven successful for me and for thousands of my students the world over. Want to know what to say when the client says, "I want to think it over?" Well, the answer to this and many more of the most common stalls is found here.

Chapter 4

The No-Frills Close

*E*very now and then, a sale closes so smoothly and quickly that it may surprise you. You just never know which potential future client will realize that you're just the right person with exactly the product he's been looking for — and he's as excited to own your product as you are to sell it. In this chapter, I cover those easy situations in which you need do little more than be professional and ask politely for their signature on paperwork or for their cash, check, or credit card.

 I've seen these easy closes happen even with large purchases. Heck, it happened with a home I once showed. The people just knew it was their dream home the moment we pulled up to the curb. They practically ran through the house and then insisted that I call the seller right away with an offer so no one else could get the home before they did. I was quite surprised at this turn of events and got caught up in their excitement. (Of course, I still made them sit down and go over the details of the transaction and then called the seller.)

 Here's a tip: With an easy close, don't act surprised in front of the clients. If they see that you're surprised, they may think they missed something in the details about the product or the financing and start second-guessing themselves, unclosing the sale just as quickly as it closed.

The Basic Oral (Verbal) Close

The basic oral close is nothing more than a question you ask that calls for a commitment to go ahead. The basic oral close is by far the simplest, easiest, and best close to master. When this close works, you're in hog heaven. If it doesn't, you've committed no fouls, and you can attempt to close another way.

Purchase order number?

This type of basic oral close is often used in industrial, commercial, and governmental sales to get purchase order numbers (which makes the sale concrete).

> By the way, what purchase order number will be assigned to this requisition?

If the customer says he doesn't know, ask:

> How do we find out?

After you have the purchase order number, it's always wise to ask if there's anyone else who needs to approve the purchase order. I'd hate to see one of your orders canceled because the decision maker needed to get a second approval on the paperwork and you just didn't know about it.

In my company, we have a check and balance system where each purchase order has two lines for approval signatures. Be sure to look at any purchase order you're given to be certain that you have the correct approval or approvals before going ahead with arranging delivery. Some companies have tiny initial lines where the next manager up the line needs to put his or her okay. For some large purchases, the chief financial officer needs to put a seal of approval on the purchase order. Just be aware of the possibilities and never hesitate to ask for clarification on the company's internal systems for making purchases.

Cash, check, or charge?

This is the simplest form of a close, especially in a retail setting — the words for the basic oral close may go like this:

> Will this be a credit card, check, or cash purchase?

With these basic oral closes, if the client hesitates, you're still okay. You haven't hurt the relationship. You haven't raised additional concerns. You've just set the stage for further closing to take place. For example, your customer may not have everything they came in for and this gives you an opportunity to increase the amount of their order. Or the customer may not have decided for sure on the purchase. If that's the case, ask what his concerns are, try to address them, and then close again.

The Basic Written Close

The basic written close has also been called the "let me make a note of that" close. You typically use this close when your paperwork requires a lot of details like measurements, choice of finishes, colors, or unusual delivery or billing requirements.

Here are some of the details you may need to get on your paperwork. You can ask questions and "make a note of that" to get your entire agreement filled out, with their permission. (I discuss asking for permission in more detail in the Obtaining permission section later in this chapter.)

- ✔ Names, with correct spelling
- ✔ Shipping address
- ✔ Billing address, if different
- ✔ Vital statistics
- ✔ Social security number
- ✔ Phone and fax numbers
- ✔ Required delivery date
- ✔ Product or service specifications — size, color, shape, texture, fabric, and so on

You can usually justify asking for any information that needs to be on your form by saying that you want the form to do its job when it leaves your hands. After all, unless you're also the one performing the service or packing the shipment, you need to relay all of this vital information to the person who fills the order so the client gets exactly what he wants and needs.

Don't ask rapid-fire questions like you're interrogating the customer for the crime of the century. Simply make sure you work all the required details into your conversation during the presentation and preparation for the close.

Does that come with a swing set?

I use the basic written close a lot in real estate to cover concerns about items being included in the purchase, such as drapes, swing sets, refrigerators, and custom-built furniture.

Any one of these items can be what makes or breaks the sale — I always found it interesting how many swing sets I sold that had homes that came with them.

Obtaining permission

The key to the basic written close is getting permission to take notes early in your presentation so you don't miss any pertinent details. By obtaining permission, I mean to ask the potential client for their permission to take notes, which is a strategic move. By giving you permission to take notes, the customers are saying that they're okay with seeing you write down stuff. Do this up front so there isn't a knee jerk, whoa-wait-a-minute reaction when you start writing on the paperwork — as there may be if you never write a lick until it's time to get serious.

Follow these steps to obtain permission from your client and have a smooth written close.

To be prepared, you need to have something to take notes with. I recommend a nice pen and a portfolio that holds a legal pad of paper and your agreement — or whatever paperwork is necessary to complete the transaction.

1. **Ask the customer for permission to take notes.**

> Would you mind if, while we chat, I jot down a few notes?

2. **When you come to any concrete detail that needs to be included on your paperwork, say:**

> Let me make a note of that.

3. Write the pertinent details on your agreement, or if the customer seems uncomfortable with that, on one of your blank note pages.

If the clients show any discomfort with your taking notes, simply remind them of the value of taking notes:

> Them: What are you writing? I'm not ready to go
>   ahead with an order yet!
>
> You: I organize my thoughts to keep everything in
>   the proper perspective. I do that on the paper-
>   work so I don't forget anything — particularly
>   anything that could cost you time or money.

What're the customers going to say to this? That they don't care about losing time or money? Of course not. After all, you haven't asked them to sign anything. (Asking for their signature is the last thing you do.) Demonstrating that you're a detail-oriented professional only shows your level of competence.

Double-checking

After you have all the details covered, take a moment to review the paperwork.

- ✔ Is the paperwork legible?

    Writing legibly is very important. You can't expect anyone to authorize illegible paperwork when making a purchase.

- ✔ Are there any details missing that can cause a delay in the processing of the order?

- ✔ Is the information correct according to instructions from the buyer?

After you've checked everything, turn the paperwork around toward the clients and hand them a pen. Ask them to review the details to be certain you have everything correct. Then say:

> With your approval right here (point to signature line), I'll
> welcome you to our family of satisfied clients and get
> started on serving your needs.

ANECDOTE

The "let me make you famous" close

If you've established good rapport and are having a somewhat light and fun time with your clients, you may wish to use this strategy that one of my students came up with. He sells recreational vehicles in Texas. When his paperwork is completed, he turns it around to his clients, hands them the pen, and says, "Let me make you famous for a moment and ask for your autograph." If there's any tension at all, this usually breaks it and guess what — they sign!

Now you shut up. Give the customers an opportunity to review the paperwork and approve it. Waiting may be tense, but resist the urge to speak. Just let the decision-making opportunity hang.

The Assumptive Close

If you've done everything properly and you know in your heart of hearts that your product or service is truly good for this person, group, or company, but you sense hesitation, use an *assumptive close,* meaning all you do is act and speak as if the customer's going ahead with the purchase.

CHAMPION STRATEGY #1

> After you complete this beauty regimen for a week, you'll see wonderful results. Your skin will be softer, and your loved ones will ask what you've been doing different to take care of yourself. You'll look better and feel better about yourself, too. By the way, did you want the basic cleansing kit or the enhanced beauty system?

You're not giving the customer a choice of whether or not she wants the beauty products. She just needs to decide which package she'll walk out the door with.

The assumptive close has also been called the *secondary question close*. If the customer agrees to the secondary question (in this case, basic kit or enhanced system), the first part (ownership of your product) is automatic. Following are a few tips to help you master the assumptive close.

✔ State the major or primary decision in terms of benefit to the client.

✔ Avoid pausing between the benefit statement and your secondary question.

✔ State the secondary question in the form of an alternate advance question.

In Chapter 5, I cover alternate advance questions in detail, but as a preview here, they are questions with two answers. Either answer moves you closer toward the decision to go ahead.

✔ Keep your attitude casual.

Mastering multiple closes

If every no-frills close has a fairly high success ratio, why should you even consider learning more than the basics? Hey, if all sales could be closed as easily as indicated in this chapter, everyone would want to be in sales because every salesperson would be a millionaire.

I recommend learning as many closes as you possibly can because you'll encounter every possible type of decision maker and situation in your sales career. In fact, a change in the selling climate can occur within one single transaction. Statistics have shown that the average closed sale requires five closing attempts, which means that the average salesperson needs to know at least five closes. You'll quickly fall to less-than-average status if you only know two or three closes. And less-than-average status means you earn a less-than-average income — and who wants that? (Obviously, no one who invests his or her time reading this book — like you.)

If there were one or two closes that worked all the time, everyone would master them. They would be used a million times a day and every customer maker on the planet would see them coming a mile away. And then the closes wouldn't be any good any more. See my point? You've gotta stay fresh. You've gotta stay in shape by mastering as many closes as you can get your hands on.

Mastery of multiple closes is the best way to keep yourself fresh, to keep your options open, and to keep closing more sales.

Bridging between Closes

Say you tried to close and the clients still came up with something to keep them from making an immediate decision. That's okay. No harm, no foul. If they haven't ended the conversation or walked out the door, you're still in the game. You just need to address their concern and bridge to another close.

Building closing bridges doesn't require a degree in engineering, but it does require you to delve deeply into your courtesy skills, and then go back to your professional selling skills. Here's your basic bridge-building blueprint:

1. **Apologize.**

   Whether or not you've done something that requires an apology doesn't matter. What does matter is that your potential client may have been feeling a little or a lot of pressure when you asked your first closing question. As with any apology, the faster and simpler it is, the better:

> I'm sorry. I thought you were ready to go ahead with the purchase. I didn't mean to rush you. Are there other concerns we haven't covered yet?

2. **Address concerns they brought up and/or answer their questions.**

Summarizing with questions

After you feel you've covered everything (once again), begin a summary review of everything the customers have agreed to thus far, including the new points just covered. Don't rush this part. Your goal is to just get them agreeing on the minor points with tie downs and statements, so you can move onto the major point of ownership. *Tie downs* are simple questions that are added to statements of fact, which call for an agreement from the client. (See Chapter 5 for the lowdown on tie downs.) Here are a few examples of tie downs:

> This model has a little more capacity than you need, so it can handle your growing needs, correct?

or

> The product will fit fine in the space you've allotted for it, right?

or

> We've agreed that you're comfortable with the financing arrangements, haven't we?

Beware of using too many tie down questions in a row, as it will become redundant. Yes, you need tie downs for summarizing, but hopefully, after you get them started, the customers will start listing things they've agreed to along with you, and you can simply nod in agreement.

Asking a lead-in question

After you've completed your summary review, get the clients to agree that you've covered everything they can think of with these words:

> Those are all the things we've discussed so far, and we have agreed on all of them, correct?

When they say yes, go for the close again. You may be able to use the same closing phrase as before.

> With your approval right here, I'll schedule your order for delivery and immediately begin serving all your needs.

Asking for their approval tells the customers that you're back to decision time again. However, if you feel you must approach the close differently, try one of the other methods recommended in this chapter and in Chapters 6, 7, and 8.

If they disagree after your summary review, ask them to clarify what it is that's missing from your summary. Perhaps they've thought of something else that you didn't cover, but needs to be addressed.

The single most important advice I can give you on closing — whether it's using a simple close like those in this chapter or the more complicated closes that Chapters 5 through 8 discuss — is just ask. The number one reason customers don't buy is because they feel they were never asked. Never, never, *never* leave your potential clients without clearly and succinctly asking for the sale.

Chapter 5

Questioning and Listening Strategies

In This Chapter

▶ Understanding the four types of questions

▶ Discovering ten useful questioning principles

▶ Figuring out how to be a better listener

A s a young person, did you ever have this experience? You're talking with an adult — say it's at Thanksgiving — and you're catching up with old Uncle Joe and he says, "Hey, Sally, you know you're quite the talker. You should go into sales. You'd be great at it." Well, Uncle Joe has a stereotypical view of what salespeople are all about — talking their way into closed sales. The average salesperson may be all babble, but you're not striving to be average. So, this chapter is about the talk — namely, the questions — champions use to close sales, and just as important, the listening tactics of champion closers. After you ask the question, you have to listen to the answer.

Champion salespeople know that the best way to a successful close is to ask questions and to listen.

Questioning Your Clients

Although nearly all children ask questions, somewhere along the road of life, people stop asking. Or they ask fewer questions. Some teenagers and adults even get to the point where they think it makes them look stupid to ask questions. I firmly believe that the only stupid question there can be is the one that's never asked.

There are many different types of questions that professional salespeople must know, and they also need to know what function each question has and when to use them in the selling sequence. The most commonly used questions are

- ✔ Discovery questions
- ✔ Leading questions

> ✔ Involvement questions
>
> ✔ Closing questions

The following sections are devoted to these questioning strategies — what they are, when they are used, and how they affect your ability to come to a successful close.

When you get really good with your questioning strategies, you're able to combine several types of questions into one. For example, you can ask a leading question that enables you to discover a lot of information in the process. When you begin to ask questions in this manner, you save a lot of time and become very targeted in the information you glean from your customers.

Discovery questions

Discovery questions are ones that help you find out more about your client and his or her needs with regard to your product or service. Discovery questions tend to be pretty automatic with most salespeople. Wanting to find out all the information possible about your prospective customers is only natural. You need to keep in mind a few rules when asking these types of questions, though.

When forming your discovery questions, remember that you're trying to gather information, so ask questions that create explanations and further discussion. Most of the time, yes-or-no responses are not what you're after. In fact, there's really no room in the discovery process to ask a question that can be answered with a no.

Never ask a "no" question during the discovery process.

Here's some of the information you need to discover:

> ✔ What product and/or service do the customers own now?
>
> ✔ What would the customers change about the product and/or service they currently own?
>
> ✔ When will the customers be looking to own their new product and/or service?
>
> ✔ What is the one feature the customers find most attractive about the new model?

Oftentimes, the best discovery questions don't end with a question mark, but instead come out like statements. For example, "I understand you use a great deal of PVC piping" isn't really a question. By posing the question like this, the customers are encouraged to talk to you. In fact, statements are a much more controlled and targeted technique of discovery.

Asking discovery questions can take awhile because you're asking the customers for information they have to explain, so be patient.

Leading questions

Leading questions are questions that help you steer the conversation to the information that helps you determine if your product is right for your client — these questions guide and convince. Many salespeople are tempted to tell their prospective customers what to believe instead of asking questions that allow the customers to come up with their own belief statements. The difference is subtle, but important. If you say it, they can doubt it; if they say it, they believe it's true! Here are some examples:

- ✔ What was it that brought you to our location today?
- ✔ What are your fitness goals?
- ✔ What type of decor do you have in mind for your new home?
- ✔ How are you currently handling your financial planning needs?

Salespeople who are unfamiliar with asking leading questions crowd the conversation with facts, feature functions, warranty information, and delivery possibilities, during which the prospective customers draw farther and farther away. Instead of the customers being lead toward a successful close, they're being pushed back against the wall. When this happens, one of two things will occur: Either the customer will take a firm stand on their own principles, or they'll melt into the woodwork and stop asking questions all together. No matter which of the two types of behavior they display, at that point, you've killed the possibility of a close.

Instead of forcing the customers' hands, gently lead and guide them toward your way of thinking by making statements regarding your product or service, then tying them down with contractions like "isn't it," "don't you agree," and "wouldn't you" to get them to agree with you. (More on tie downs in the following section.)

- ✔ The particular shade of blue in this blouse sets off the blue of your eyes, don't you think?
- ✔ The latest safety features are vital when considering the safety of your daughter in her first new car, aren't they?
- ✔ Having a solid financial plan is a wise move when you have a family to think of, don't you agree?

Be sure you know what you want the answers to be before you ask the questions, and be sure your customers know the answers as well. Nobody likes to be asked questions that make them feel stupid, and that certainly won't lead the customers toward a close unless it's to close the front door in your face as they leave the building!

Understanding tie downs

Tie downs are questions that you put at the end of statements that call for agreement from the client. Most tie downs are forms of leading questions, which get the clients to elaborate on their thoughts about your statements. One thing to remember, though, is to mix up the different ways of wording tie downs so the prospective customer doesn't suspect your technique. The following phrases are some common tie downs you'll find useful (see the following section, "Placing tie downs in a sentence," for where and how to use them):

- ✔ Aren't they?
- ✔ Don't we?
- ✔ Isn't it?
- ✔ Didn't it?
- ✔ Aren't you?
- ✔ Shouldn't it?
- ✔ Isn't that right?
- ✔ Wasn't it?
- ✔ Can't you?
- ✔ Wouldn't it?
- ✔ Haven't they?
- ✔ Won't they?
- ✔ Couldn't it?
- ✔ Hasn't he?
- ✔ Hasn't she?
- ✔ Won't you?
- ✔ Doesn't it?
- ✔ Don't you agree?
- ✔ Can't you just imagine?

Customize the tie down to each situation. Remember, the more creative you can be, the more effectively you'll lead the customers to a close.

Placing tie downs in a sentence

You can sneak tie downs into just about any sentence:

✔ **Standard tie down:** Placed at the end of the sentence.

> A company's reputation is important when choosing a firm to do business with, isn't it?

or

> Your children will be pretty excited about all the fun times they'll have on this new boat, won't they?

or

> You'll sleep better at night knowing that your property is protected by a top notch security system, won't you?

✔ **Inverted tie downs:** Used at the beginning of a sentence. The inverted tie down can make your questions sound a little warmer.

> Can't you just picture yourself sitting by the fireplace on a cold winter's night?

or

> Isn't it about time you treated your family to the vacation of a lifetime?

or

> Shouldn't you be offered the highest return by placing your securities in ABC Bank?

✔ **Internal tie downs:** Placed in the middle of a sentence. Internal tie downs are actually the smoothest way to hide the fact that you are using a technique and make it sound like you're asking a matter-of-fact, I-just-thought-of-this question.

> This new computer game is fun, isn't it, once you get everything loaded.

or

> Because you're planning on delivery by the middle of June, don't you think that ordering now would be a good idea?

or

> Now that we've eliminated that concern, don't you agree that we can move forward in the building process?

✔ **Tag-on tie downs:** Add-on sentences. Tag-on tie downs are used when your prospective customer makes a positive statement that you want to reinforce.

> Them: The Copier 2000 can certainly crank out the copies.
>
> You: Can't it though?

or

> Them: This Corvette is incredibly fast!
>
> You: Isn't it?

or

> **Them:** I'll be so glad to never have to wash another dish by hand!
>
> **You:** Can't you just imagine??

The key with tag-on tie downs is that they must be used only after the prospective customer has made a positive statement about your offering. Be patient. Wait for those positive statements to pop up and then tie them down with a tag-on tie down.

Closing questions

A closing question is one that calls for a decision on the purchase. When non-customers are asked why they didn't purchase a product, most of those who liked the product said they didn't purchase it because they were never asked! Hard to believe, isn't it? Salepeople would never want to admit that they don't ask closing questions, but some salespeople are uncomfortable asking people for their money and will dance around the issue, never asking a customer — point blank — if he wants to own the product.

Some salespeople may say things like: "So what do you think?" Or, "It's a good product, isn't it?" Even though the client may agree with them, they never actually ask for the money, the credit card, or the approval on the paperwork. Closing questions sound more like this: "How would you like to cover the investment for your new window coverings?" Or, "With your approval right here (indicating signature line of paperwork), we'll get a delivery date set so you can begin enjoying your new entertainment system." In retail sales, the most common close is this: "Will this be cash, check, or charge?" Is the client asked to buy the product? You bet. After you have confirmation from a closing question, do what the professionals do — close.

You may be surprised at how many salespeople keep on asking more closing questions when, in reality, they've already received a yes. Check out the following sections, which examine a few closing questions and show how and when to use them.

The alternate advance

The *alternate advance question* gives the prospective customers a choice of a positive answer or a "yes" answer. The idea behind this is that either way, the customers indicate their intentions to own. These types of questions are never merely yes-or-no questions, but require a choice instead.

Here's how the alternate advance question works. Instead of asking the customer if you can come by to show him your product, use the following instead (you're much less likely to get a no from the customer):

> Would Tuesday morning be a good time for me to drop by, or is Wednesday more convenient for you?

Can you hear the difference? See how much easier it is for the customer to say no to you when just you ask if you can stop by? And how, by asking what time is best for you to drop by, you force the customer away from a simple "no" answer?

If you were asking a question that requires an investment from your prospective customer, word it like this:

> The people we serve have found it a good idea to reserve their vacation spot by placing a deposit; would you prefer 5 or 10 percent as an initial investment?

Alternate advance questions simply allow salespeople to avoid getting that "no" answer. Keep in mind that if you ask a question that can be answered by either a yes or a no response, you may well get a "no" — and a boot to the door.

The porcupine technique

The *porcupine technique* is one of the strongest forms of closing questions, but like the tie downs, customers will suspect if the porcupine technique is overused. You use this technique when customers ask you a question and you need to establish where they stand on the issue, so you counter their question with one of your own. The reason this type of closing question is called the porcupine technique is because no one wants to hold a porcupine for very long. Throw the porcupine (question) back immediately, before you get stabbed by a flying quill you hadn't counted on. The following scenario is one in which you'd use the porcupine technique.

> Them: Is there a park nearby?
>
> You: Is it important to you to have a park near your home?

Rather than using the porcupine technique to see where the customer stood before answering, the salesperson could have immediately come back with a response like:

You'll love the park that is less than two houses down. It's a great place for the kids to play, and you can keep an eye on them.

This seems like a reasonable response, right? Well, look at it this way. What if the customer had no children and didn't want the noise and traffic that a park would add to the neighborhood? By immediately assuming that the customer would like the park, you just killed your chances for a successful close.

Don't assume you know the customer's likes and dislikes. Instead, use the porcupine technique to feel out the customer.

Involvement questions

An *involvement question* is any positive question about the benefits of your product or service that buyers would ask themselves after they own it. Involvement questions let you know exactly where your prospective customers stand on the idea of owning your product.

If you were to go ahead, where in the office would you put the soda machine?

The soda machine would have to be conveniently located for his employees, so the customer pictures the flow of traffic in the office and see people using the machine.

Do you think your furniture would fit well in this room?

By asking this, you cause the customer to visualize the furniture in his home.

> How often do you think you'll be entertaining after having the patio improvements made?

Here the customer starts picturing a party and how he'd set it all up.

Involvement questions are usually a combination of leading, discovery, and closing questions all wrapped into one. Involvement questions require a bit more finesse and planning in order to achieve the positive results you are looking for, but practice makes perfect.

Ten pointers for successful questioning

Here are ten pointers on questioning strategies. If diligently applied, they will almost always move you to a successful close.

Ask how you can help

When you first meet potential new clients, you need to ask questions to determine just what you can do for them. The single best question for this strategy is this:

> How can I help you?

You're not asking whether or not you can help the customers — you know you *can* help them. You want to know *how* you can help them. With this question, you're figuring out specifically how you can serve the customers' needs. In order to serve, they must tell you their needs — and this is a good question to get the ball rolling.

The answer to this question may tell you that you can't help them today. For example, if you sell playground equipment, people may stop by your location just to see what kinds of fun things you have and their only child is just three months old. You probably can't be of service to them today. You want to determine that rather quickly, make them feel good about your products, and then let them browse and leave with brochures. Then, you can make yourself available to the next group that pulls in with four children under the age of eight.

Determine specific benefits

In qualifying and presenting, use this strategy to narrow down your offering from the many options you have to give the prospective client. Determining specific features and benefits is helpful in the information gathering stage of the sale; however, it's also used to close the sale.

> Did you want the bay window on the north side of the living room or on the east?

or

> That set comes in a choice of colors. Would the Bluejay Blue go better on your patio or the Grassyknoll Green?

or

> There are several solutions we can provide your company. Let me ask you which is more important to you in providing a new health care plan: a wide range of benefits to meet the myriad of needs your people have or a more narrow range that is available at a lower investment?

As part of your closing summary, reiterate all the things that your customer told you he wanted up to this point. This shows you were paying attention, that you can keep track of details, and that you're covering all his needs effectively. After he agrees to this review, you ask your closing question.

Acknowledge the facts

You can do more with questions than just ask about the client's needs. You can state a fact as a question and get his agreement. If your product involves a warranty, ask early on if having a warranty is important to the client. If it isn't, you don't bring it up again. However, if it is important, bring it up in the form of a question to get your client in the agreement mode as you prepare to close the sale.

> You said that the 10-year extended warranty was important to you, wasn't it?

When your client agrees with you on this point, you can confirm that he's going ahead. After all, he wouldn't agree to wanting the warranty if he wasn't serious about getting the product or service, right?

You then proceed to the next step in the selling sequence, which is to review all the financial details. If the client's agreeable to all of that, ask for his approval on the paperwork or whatever form of payment he's using.

Test their level of commitment

If you're not sure how strong the customers' desire is to go ahead after you've given them all of the details about the product or service, ask!

You test their level of interest or desire to go ahead with what I call *trial* or *test closes,* which are covered more in depth in Chapter 2. Test closes are simply a matter of testing how the customers feel at this moment about everything you've covered — kind of like taking the temperature of the sale.

> How are you feeling about everything we've discussed so far?

An example test question like this one gets your clients to let you know whether they're for, against, or indifferent to what they've discovered about your product and how it suits their needs.

- ✔ If they're for owning the product, proceed with your benefit summary, review of the financial details, and close.

- ✔ If they're against it, ask them to elaborate on how they're feeling, so that you can find out what's holding them back.

- ✔ If they're indifferent, you'll need to ask more questions about their needs. Use tie downs to review the points they've agreed to and confirm that they want those benefits. Ask if there is anything else that may be keeping them from making a decision. When they're indifferent, something is missing. You have to find out what's missing and get it covered — you do that by asking questions.

Arouse emotions

Arousing and directing emotions can be tricky. You want to be certain that you're arousing the right emotions for the situation.

As an example, if you're selling home security products you can ask:

> Won't you sleep better on the road next week, knowing that your wife, children, and pets are protected by our security team?

With this question, you help the customer picture his family and pets sleeping peacefully and protected — which conjures a positive emotion. He'll also feel less guilty about being gone overnight.

Don't try to raise emotions when discussing the money aspects of the sale. Most people will conjure up negative images about money leaving their hands for good. For example, don't say, "Won't you feel great knowing this $200 per month is going toward little Johnnie's college education?" The client may picture little Johnnie needing new shoes because he's growing so fast and how expensive shoes really are and begin to feel over-whelmed about his responsibility as a parent and so on. When you're talking about money, stick to the facts and figures unless money is the final objection. If it is, then you may want to tie it to something emotional that the client may miss out on by not going ahead today (like little Johnnie's college graduation ceremony).

(I cover how to overcome money objections in greater detail in Chapter 6.)

Get the minor yeses flowing

To get minor yeses, get them agreeing on minor points. Minor agreements accumulate into major ones, and that's where you want to end up — with a major agreement! I love using the following question for getting a minor yes:

> This brand of furniture has an excellent reputation for quality, and quality is important when making a purchase of this sort, isn't it?

Are they going to disagree with that? Nope. You've just gotten a minor agreement. You know that name brand furniture is what they want. Most clients know that name brand means quality, and that quality means a higher financial investment. This minor yes gives you a foundation for knowing how much they may be willing to invest in the furniture they're discussing with you. From this point, narrow down their specific needs to pieces, styles, finishes — all the details. After they choose what they want, you can cover the money.

Involve your customers in ownership

This strategy is to get your prospective clients picturing themselves owning your product or service.

✔ If your product is something tangible, such as a car, you can ask questions about placement of it after ownership. In other words, where will it reside? Do they have garage space for it? Will it be parked on the street? If so, would they be interested in having a security alarm as an added-on feature? Ask who will be using the car. If it's a spouse with small children, discuss safety with them. If it's a teen, perhaps the cost of insurance is foremost on their minds — if the safety features of a particular model lend to receiving better insurance rates, you may want to bring that up. Get the picture? Ask how the customers think it will look, feel, and work. Ask how the car will benefit them and their loved ones.

✔ If your product is intangible, you have to help customers picture themselves owning the benefits of it. If your product is a cleaning service, help them see themselves relaxing instead of cleaning — walking into a clean home at the end of a busy day. If your product is insurance, help them see themselves covered in an unfortunate instance.

The more you help customers feel ownership of your product or service, the less closing you have to do later.

Isolate areas of concern

Say your clients have been going over a new insurance plan with you. They've brought up a few points along the way that could be considered objections. (I prefer to call objections *concerns*. In my mind, the word "objection" is too harsh — like a lawyer jumping up out of his chair and yelling out the word to save his client's life.) You need to isolate their areas of concern before you can move to the close.

Concerns are simply points that need to be addressed or read-dressed to make your client comfortable enough to make a buying decision. Customer concerns generally fall into three categories:

- ✔ Will your product or service really do what you say it will?
- ✔ Is this truly the best product for us, for our particular situation?
- ✔ Do we really want to spend the money on this?

In my experience, the third point — the money — is the final area of concern that you have to address in 90 percent of closing situations. However, the other 10 percent cannot be ignored unless you want to be only 90 percent of a champion or meet 90 percent of your quota or earn 90 percent of what you could potentially earn. The other 10 percent relates to whether or not the product will perform as expected and if it's simply the best choice for them. If what's holding them back is faith that your product will perform, you need to pull out testimonials from happy clients or maybe give them a list of clients they can contact for referrals about the product. To show that this is the best product for them, you have to rely on your expertise regarding the products your competition offers.

To isolate the customer's primary concern, simply ask at the end of your presentation:

> So your primary concern seems to be the financial aspect of this plan. Am I correct in my understanding of that?

If something besides the money needs to be addressed, you want to know about it before you start going for the close on the money.

Make sure objections are settled

After you address a concern and you believe the customers are satisfied with the information you've given them, you need to get confirmation so the same objection doesn't come up again when it's time to close. This strategy is simple, yet powerful. After you've addressed the customers' concern and they seem comfortable, say:

> Now that settles that, doesn't it?

RED FLAG

Two key principles of questioning power

✔ Always create a bond between the prospective customer and yourself before establishing control through the questioning process.

✔ Leading people to decisions on what you're prepared to offer is impossible until you know the product and/or service that best suits their needs.

If they truly are comfortable, the customers will agree and you can move on. If the issue isn't settled, you want to find out while you're still on the topic of their concern and get it settled once and for all.

Stay in control

If you feel you're not in control of the selling situation, ask a question to bring the conversation back to the task at hand. If you sell backyard play equipment and your prospects start talking about anything and everything having to do with their kids rather than talking about your product, take control with a question:

CHAMPION STRATEGY #1

It's wonderful that your children are so active. Now, let me ask you what the specific current motor development skills are of each of your children so we can talk about customizing your equipment for their particular needs.

Bring them back to the task at hand — choosing a product — by showing how that information they've just relayed about little Susie and her soccer team or Billy and his karate relates to benefits they'll receive from your product. For intangibles, listen for something important to them in the side story and apply it to a need your product will meet. For example they're concerned about Grandma being alone, your senior monitoring service fills that void, doesn't it?

Rationalize decisions for your clients

People buy products and services emotionally and then defend the purchases logically. If you doubt this, take a look at this progression of emotion:

1. Judy is a working mom.

2. She hates spending her evenings and weekends cleaning house and doing laundry.

3. The kids are growing up quickly and she wants them to have fun memories — and she wants to be a part of those memories.

4. She decides, based on these emotions, to hire someone to clean house and do laundry for her for $50 per week.

As soon as the emotional decision is made, guilt and fear make their attack, telling Judy that $50 is a lot of money to commit to spending every week. She could take the kids on some great outings with that money. So Judy starts second-guessing herself. She needs logic to defend her decision.

How would a champion salesperson close this sale? By asking questions and rationalizing the decision for the client.

> **You:** I can see that you're hesitant to make this financial commitment. Let's think this through for a moment. How much time do you think you spend on these chores?
>
> **Them:** I probably spend at least 10 to 12 hours per week cleaning and keeping up with the laundry.
>
> **You:** Okay, let's go with 10 hours per week. Based on the amount of time you say you put into taking care of these chores, the $50 per week investment boils down to $5 per hour, which is less than minimum wage. I don't know what you earn in the working world, but don't you think your time is worth more than $5 per hour?

The spending of money has been rationalized. The cleaning service is hired, and the guilt disappears in a sprinkle of rationalized dust. The customer is more relaxed, and she feels she has more of herself to give to her family. And she's having more fun. All of this for only $50 a week.

Ask for the close

There are right and wrong ways to ask closing questions. You (obviously) don't flat out ask, "Do you want it or not?" You do, however, ask for the client's approval, okay, endorsement, or authorization on the paperwork so you can immediately begin serving their needs. We always ask in a professional, non-threatening manner, but we do ask! Never, ever, ever let yourself leave the presence of a client without asking for the sale!

In Chapters 6, 7, 8, and 9, I cover specific closing situations and the phraseology for closing the sale with each.

Listening While You Work

For most salespeople, listening just isn't the natural way to spend most of their time. Too bad, because the more you listen, the more you earn! If you doubt this, consider that many psychologists earn $95 or more per hour to listen to the challenges people face. Of course, they're providing solutions as well, but aren't you supposed to do that, too?

Here are some interesting statistics that should greatly influence your desire to become a good listener.

- ✔ Good communicators spend at least 40 percent of their time listening.

  Contrary to what you may think, during our entire formal educational experience, less than one year is devoted to learning how to listen. That's one year total, which in reality is only a few minutes here and there interspersed in 12 to 16 years of education.

- ✔ Approximately 35 percent of a good communicator's time is spent talking.

  The time in school given to developing good speaking skills is, on average, only two years.

- ✔ About 16 percent of our time is spent reading.

  Six to eight years are spent learning how to read.

- ✔ Nine percent of our communication skills is spent writing.

  Twelve years are spent learning how to write.

What do these statistics tell you? We spend a lot of time learning to do best what we will eventually use the least. As a sales professional, you should spend about 30 percent of your time talking and 30 percent prospecting, doing research, and preparing presentations. Notice that I said 30 percent talking. For many salespeople, talking less goes against the grain of what they really do. To help you remember and stick to this advice, think about the proportion of ears to mouth in the human being. We have twice as many ears as mouths, right? Use them in that proportion if you want to succeed.

You can't begin to make up for all that lost time in school, where learning effective listening skills was pushed under the carpet and believed by many to be a minor skill. You can, however, become more aware of the level of listener you are and what pitfalls may await you unless you change your ways. The great thing about changing your listening habits is that you can begin immediately and practice every day without people ever knowing what you're doing. Becoming a good listener is definitely a learned process. Read on for more information on how to become a better listener.

Three types of listeners

The following identify three major types of listeners. Take a look and see which one fits you. Evaluate what listening type you are, to what degree you fit in that particular category, and as you continue reading this chapter, think about what you can do to improve your listening skills.

  ✔ **Poor Listener.** These are the people who catch themselves picking up on a conversation that they're supposed to be a part of, realizing that they weren't focused on the other speaker. They may wonder what details, if any, were missed during their "time out," but are too embarrassed to ask the speaker to repeat himself.

  ✔ **Average Listener.** These listeners hear the words, but may not be watching the body language of the speaker or catching where the speaker puts the most emphasis, which is vital to interpreting messages that the speaker does not send verbally.

  ✔ **Empathetic Listener.** This listener pays total attention to the subject at hand. He or she is not only a good listener, but is observant as well. When the atmosphere contains many distractions, the empathetic listener is able to block them out and concentrate on what's important.

Take the following survey to see if you're an empathetic listener. Think about your most recent conversation. This conversation doesn't have to have been with a client — it could have been with a coworker or significant other.

  1. Did you listen intently to what they were saying?

  2. Did you make eye contact several times during the conversation?

  3. Did you repeat important points back to the other party to ensure that you understood them correctly?

4. Could you now accurately repeat the details of the conversation to another person?

5. Do you recall the bodily movements of the speakers? How were they standing? Or were they sitting? Were their arms crossed or open? What was their level of eye contact with you?

6. Did they repeat a point in several ways for emphasis? If they did, did you catch the importance of that point?

If you're stumped by any of these questions, you have room for improvement in your listening skills. You may want to jot down these questions on a 3 x 5 card and carry the card with you. Review the questions prior to your next conversation, and then see how you do afterward.

Your listening skills can vary by many degrees. You may even discover that your listening habits vary with whatever it is you're are focused on learning. If you're interested in what is being discussed, your focus will be greater and your attentiveness will be, too. Naturally, if you are indifferent to the topic, retaining what you hear won't be of major importance to you.

In all fairness, oftentimes the fault of poor listening habits has nothing to do with the topic; rather, the listener's inability to focus is due to fatigue, stress, or physical ailments. An incredible number of things can distract us during a day, and all those distractions interfere with our ability to listen, learn, and retain.

Getting your client's attention

When the table is turned and you're the person who wants to be listened to, what can you do to improve the habits of a poor listener? Here are seven ways to attract and maintain the attention of your listener, the customer:

✔ Make sure the room is comfortable and free of distractions.

✔ Ask questions to get the customer to communicate or relax.

To get your customers to relax, ask about a subject they're comfortable discussing to establish rapport — and keep their attention.

> I see by your cap that you're a Phoenix Suns fan. Do you go to the games?

✔ Maintain eye contact with the customer when speaking.

✔ If you see signs of the customer's attention drifting, use the customer's name in a sentence.

✔ Avoid being critical or judgmental.

✔ Watch the customer's body language. If you're losing him, suggest a break or do a brief recap where you summarize what's been discussed or agreed to up to this point. (The purpose of summarizing is to bring everyone up to the same level of understanding.) Remember to do a recap after taking a break.

✔ Don't let any visual aids you use in your presentation distract your listener. Visual aids should compliment the message — not confuse it. After you finish with a particular visual aid, put it out of sight and move on.

✔ Ask questions about what the customer has said that's relevant to your product and/or service.

Chapter 6

Closes That Overcome Fear

· ·

In This Chapter

▶ Knowing the basic fear fundamentals

▶ Taking a look at what makes your customer afraid to own

▶ Substituting the positive for the negative

▶ Getting over general fears

▶ Getting over specific fears

▶ Blending in with the emotional environment

· ·

*B*efore I really get into this chapter about overcoming the fears of your customers, you need to understand some basic information about fear in general. First and foremost, whenever you sit down with a potential client, realize that there will be someone else at the table with you, and I call him "Mr. Fear." Fear is such a powerful entity in any decision-making process that I want you to think of fear as another person involved in the situation — a very negative, devil's advocate type of person who is definitely not sitting on your side of the table. Your mission is to dissolve the fears that old Mr. Fear brings into play so that your client can make a buying decision with confidence.

Fear causes people to stall in making decisions. So be aware that any time the customer stalls, there's a fear that needs to be addressed. Many of the fears you'll encounter have been encountered by myself and other salespeople in the past. I cover those fears in this chapter so you'll be able to recognize them — and in some cases, avoid them entirely. I also show you how to handle the ones you can't avoid.

Covering the Bases: Some Fundamentals of Fear

There are certain fundamentals to understand when working with people's fears. Here's a short list:

✔ Every customer experiences some sort of fear in the decision-making process.

✔ Fear can be a direct response to something the salesperson has said or done.

✔ Fear can be from something outside the realm of the selling experience.

✔ There are some occasions where fear wins and everybody loses.

✔ The more salespeople understand fear in selling situations, the more they're able to control it and even overcome it.

I believe that experienced selling professionals — those who've had a certain degree of success — have probably earned the equivalent of a degree in psychology, just through their personal experiences. In this business, you have to gain a good understanding of how the majority of people react in pressure situations, which occur when people have to make decisions.

Figuring Out What Creates Fear in the Buyer

This section covers several things that commonly create fear in customers. By figuring out how to recognize each fear and how to respond, you can have better control over your opportunities to close sales.

Your buyer fears you

Please realize that one of the strongest things many prospective customers fear is you. You are a typical salesperson in their eyes — until you show them differently. They believe you have the single-minded goal of selling them your product or service. You know it. They know it. They raise the drawbridge and start boiling the kettles of oil the moment they agree to talk with you. They prepare to do battle, not necessarily in a confrontational manner, but the barriers do go up simply because of who and what you are — a salesperson. Your job is to make sales. You are going to try to move them to a decision they aren't sure they want to make.

So, your primary goal is to establish rapport with your customers, and let them see that you are a sales professional, not a sales stereotype. You're there to serve their needs. Of course, if making a sale serves their needs — whoopee! But if your product or service does not meet their needs, you have to show them that you won't try to persuade them to buy it anyway. In other words, you have to let your high standards of professional ethics show.

Over the past few years, many salespeople and many companies have tried to work around this common initial fear by using different titles for their profession, such as marketing executives, investment counselors, network marketers, and on and on. I'm a big believer in using non-fear-producing words (as you find out later in this chapter). If a change of title helps relax the fear barrier, go ahead and use it.

But don't ever forget that you are a salesperson! I worry that some of the titles people use instead of "salesperson" may make them stop believing that they truly are salespeople — and they end up leaving many potential clients for the competition. With their new title they become too gentle, too much like an order-taker instead of an expert advisor and sales professional whose goal is to help clients make decisions that are good for them. So remember, no matter what title you use, you're a salesperson at heart.

Your buyer fears making a mistake — again

Face it — we've all made bad decisions at one time or another in our lives. Do you think the customer you're working with has ever made a bad decision? Probably. Was he or she called on the carpet for it? Maybe. Was it a pleasant experience? Of course not. Do you think there will be a certain amount of fear about making a mistake again? Yep.

Old Mr. Fear will be happily reminding your buyers of all their bad past decisions at the same time that you're trying to show them why your product or service is just right for their current needs. If you sense a lot of hesitation in your buyers, you may want to point-blank ask them this question:

I sense some hesitation here about making this decision. Please help me to understand what you're thinking so I can best serve your needs. Can you elaborate on what your hesitation is about?

If the customer made a decision about a similar product that he has since regretted, keep him talking about it until you find out all the details. Then, demonstrate how your product and the current situation are different, building his confidence in making the right decision this time.

Your buyer fears being lied to

Many customers out there believe that a salesperson would lie to make a sale. The battle against the historical stereotype of a salesperson is something we must always fight against — unfortunately, this stereotypical image of the moneygrubbing salesperson has been perpetuated by Hollywood over the years. Until you build his confidence in your abilities to serve his needs, this fear is likely to nag at him.

Reduce this fear of being lied to by being yourself. If a question comes up that you don't know the answer to, tell the customer you don't know the answer, but that you'll find out for him as soon as the meeting is over — sooner if it's critical. This action shows him that you're not too slick. You don't make things up off the cuff. You don't lie to make the sale.

You may even encounter a customer cynical enough to say something along the lines of:

> **Them:** You salespeople are all alike. I can't trust you. You'd lie to your own mother to make a sale.

Don't let customers like this get to you. When you meet up with such a distrustful customer, respond with:

> You obviously have a reason for saying that. Would you mind elaborating on it for me?

You're not being defensive. You're showing that you care enough to hear him out. The customer's probably referring to a bad past experience that had nothing to do with you. After he's finished ranting, help him to see the difference between then and now. Then move back to the topic at hand: how your product or service will make his life better. Use testimonials or proof letters from existing clients to enhance the credibility of your company and your product.

Your buyer fears incurring debt

With the advent of the home computer and all the great software to make our lives easier, many average people can punch a key or two and bring up an in-depth analysis of their current financial status that could put some big business accounting departments to shame. There has never been a time where as many people could analyze their debt structure as there is today.

Having a good credit rating is important to any consumer or business. In order to have a good credit rating, customers have to have used some form of credit somewhere along the line. Sadly, many people have learned the hard way the perils of misusing credit. It's oh-so-easy to get into debt! Getting out of debt is another story — hundreds of thousands (perhaps millions) of people have gotten in over their heads and either filed bankruptcy or severely restricted their styles of living until they could pay down their debts. In cases such as these, it's normal for people to have a certain reluctance about incurring debt.

 If your product is large enough that most people finance its purchase, you'll face this fear on a daily basis. Your job is to build the value of your product or service to the degree where not having the product is more uncomfortable than not having the money.

Your buyer fears losing face

Losing face with your industry peers can be suicidal to your career. Purchasing agents are responsible for up to millions of dollars' worth of purchases each year. A few bad decisions and their credibility — and probably much of their authority — goes out the window. A bad decision may even lead to finding a new career. Even if they remain as purchasing agents, tales of their big embarrassment are bound to resurface every now and again. No one wants to be in this type of situation.

Granted, not too many individuals are responsible for millions of dollars; however, everyone wants to know that the money they spend is spent wisely. No one wants to be the butt of family jokes about their supposed great deal way back in '58 (or whenever). Those stories go on forever and are handed down through the generations — it's not what anyone wants to be remembered for. Your customers don't want to lose face with their peers or their relatives.

If your product is new or on the forefront of what is predicted to be a trend, there will be a certain degree of risk for anyone getting involved. The risk may or may not be financial; it may be a risk of credibility. In these potentially high-risk situations, you need to work extra hard to develop the customer's confidence in you and your product.

Your buyer fears the unknown

Fear of the unknown makes a lot of sense. Unless — and until — you have a good understanding of something, self-protecting fears instinctively arise in you at the thought of the unknown. So if this is the first time your prospective client has considered a purchase of your sort of product, be ready to address his fear of the unknown. You'll have to gently and enthusiastically educate him about your offering. Include statistics, testimonials, and as much hands-on experience as possible. You're the teacher, so be creative with your "classroom" technique.

After your customers are educated or experienced with regard to a product or service, they can relax — their fear of the unknown will begin to dissipate. You should be able to observe this transition quite easily as your potential clients start asking questions to clarify their understanding of what your product or service can do for them.

Your buyer's fear is based on bad past experiences

Prospective customers vividly remember what happened to them in past selling situations — the bad ones in particular. If they had a bad experience with someone selling copiers and you're here to show them the new and improved model to replace their malfunctioning one, chances are good they won't see you when you first walk in. They'll see that other salesperson who sold them a machine that couldn't hold up.

When the negative past experience was with a salesperson from your company, you're going to have to work twice as hard. In this situation, the customer not only doubts the product, they doubt your company. What I call the old "put the shoe on their foot" strategy works really well in a situation with a cranky client. You simply ask the client how he'd handle the situation if he were the person in charge.

CHAMPION STRATEGY
#1

Them: The last guy I talked with from your company actually recommended this piece of junk we're having to replace. I don't know if I even want to discuss this purchase with you.

> You: I can understand your concern. Would you, for just a moment, pretend that you're the president of XYZ Company and you've just found out that a representative of yours made a poor recommendation to a valued client? What would you do?
>
> Them: I'd have the #%$@ jerk fired or at least put back through product training so he didn't make the same mistake again. Then, I'd send my best person out to try to make amends with the client.

At this point, you warmly smile and say:

> You: That's probably just what happened because I've been sent here to you today to help you resolve this situation. We at XYZ Company want you to have the finest quality copier that will meet your needs not only today, but as your business grows in the future. Please tell me more about your needs.

If the client's bad past experience was with another company, you won't have to work as hard to become the hero. You will, however, find yourself under a good bit of scrutiny as the client does his best to avoid another bad experience. (Take a look at the section "The make it better close" in this chapter for more on how to handle the customer with a past.)

Your buyer's fear is based on prejudice

Being prejudiced about a product and/or service (or even toward a company or salesperson) is usually based on ignorance.

I know of a man who won't even consider owning a particular make of vehicle because while he was growing up, his father had a bad experience with a car made by this certain auto manufacturer. The problem may have been a freak incident. Or maybe the problem was resolvable at the time, but it just wasn't handled to the father's satisfaction. However, as far as this guy is concerned, this make of vehicle is not the vehicle for him — he's blindly prejudiced. Does it make sense that he still feels this way more than 20 years later? No. But he feels it just the same.

If you represent any brand of merchandise, you're bound to encounter someone who is prejudiced against your brand. Overcoming this kind of fear requires you to not only prove yourself, but to also provide proof that you, your company, and your product or service will do what you say you will. Then you have to do the hard part: deliver!

On the up side of customers' prejudice, you'll also encounter people who won't consider owning any other brand than the one you represent because it's what they grew up with. Your product is what their whole family uses, and a competitor would be hard-pressed to get these customers to consider making a change.

Your buyer's fear is based on third party information

Many times your prospective customers may be consulting a third party for advice and this third party can't seem to bring itself to a decision. Or, if the third party does come to a decision, it isn't in your favor. In this case, Mr. Fear has brought in reinforcements.

Are you aware that a third party almost always says no when the decision maker presents the information on the product he wants to buy? For example, say the decision makers are a young couple and they consult with their parents. Inevitably, after consulting with parents, they'll come back to you with a negative response. Why? People are always going to be safe by saying no. If the third party encourages you to own and then things go wrong, who do you think will feel responsible for your loss? Yep, the third party — the people who gave you the go-ahead — will. The suggestions of friends or family members that you shouldn't make a purchase is human nature. They don't want to hurt you, so they figure no action is better than taking action on advice that ends up being wrong.

You need to build the decision makers' confidence in your product enough that they don't feel the need to consult a third party. You also have to build their confidence in themselves so they feel they can make a wise decision without outside assistance.

Your buyer's fear is increased by negative images

In *Selling for Dummies*, I go into detail on how what you say creates pictures in the minds of your buyers. Think about it. When you hear the word "dog," do you see the word *dog* in your mind? Probably not. Most people visualize a dog, not the word. With the visual image, they experience a positive or negative reaction depending on whether or not they like dogs. Now think about the words you use when you're attempting to close the sale. If you use any words that can possibly create negative images in the minds of your buyers, you have to work harder to close the sale. Create a strong enough negative image and there'll be no way you can make the sale. I call these negative, fear-producing words *rejection words*. Figuring out how to replace rejection words with words that build positive images will help you close more sales. Read on for more on replacing the negative with the positive.

Replacing Rejection Words with Go-Ahead Terms

As I discuss in the preceding section, a *rejection word* is any word that triggers fear or reminds prospects that you're trying to sell them. Rejection words are closing killers. When you let a rejection word slip, selling to the customer often becomes a slow, painful process. Rejection words scare your prospects so much that most of them will reject you and your product or service. Before you even realize what's happened, the possibilities of a successful close shrivel up and die right in front of you. If you don't control rejection words — the words that conjure up negative responses and images in buyers' minds — the only close you'll experience will be the door in your face as your prospective customers make a quick exit.

Each of the following sections lists a word or phrase that you need to immediately drop from your selling vocabulary if you want to be a master closer. To help you on your way, I provide more positive words to replace the rejection words, along with some sample dialogue to show the positive words in action.

Objection

Objection is yesterday's word. Today's objections are referred to as *concerns* or *areas of concern.*

When you hear or use the term *objection,* you likely hear in your mind an attorney in a courtroom drama shouting out, "Your honor, I object!" Then what happens? All dialogue comes to a halt while the judge makes a call as to whether or not to include that last juicy tidbit as admissible evidence.

The term *concern* is softer. It's something for everyone to consider, not just the judge. A concern may sidetrack the main theme of conversation for a bit, but it doesn't halt progress. The client is concerned, so you're concerned and you commit to addressing that concern. An objection is like throwing down the gauntlet. It presents too antagonistic an image.

I understand your concern about that point; with your permission, I'd like to make a note of it and, we'll cover it at the end of my presentation.

Cheaper

Talk about stirring up emotions. Never let the customers hear the word *cheaper*. Not many people really want cheap goods or services in the context of *cheap* meaning *less than*.

Our product is so much cheaper than that of any of our competitors.

The next thing that comes to my mind after a statement like that is the question, "Why? Is it of lesser quality? Do you have an overstock because no one wants them? Why? Why? Why?"

Referring to your product or service as more *economical* lends itself to more of a positive impression. It's a wise thing to be economical.

Not only is our product of the highest quality, but it's much more economical than most brand name models.

Closing room

You'd think professional salespeople would have graduated beyond using the phrase *closing room*. Just imagine the picture those words create in the mind of the prospective client:

Let's finish up right over here in the closing room.

Using the phrase "closing room" will create an emotional response all right, but it isn't going to be the emotion that leads to a successful close. More likely, the customers will feel like you're taking them into a cell for holding until they cough up the cash.

Use the term *presentation room* or *conference room* instead:

> Our conference room **is much more comfortable and private. Follow me, won't you?**

See how much better this sounds?

Customers

Customer is a difficult word to stop using when you're with your clients. After all, customer is a word you commonly use in private conversations with fellow salespeople.

Customers creates an impersonal categorization of people. Why risk having a potential new client feel that he'll become just one of hundreds of others in a statistic?

Serving others is really what selling is all about. The best way to stop using this word is to think of the customer as someone you are *serving:*

> The people we serve **in the Phoenix area truly enjoy the benefits of our product.**

or

> Did you realize **that we** serve **over 25 families in this neighborhood already?**

Lookers

Your clients are never just *lookers;* they are *researchers.* For example, if a young couple came into a furniture store, a professional salesperson would approach them as if they were researching what living room set would look best in their new home — not as if they were there to just look around.

If you assume or even risk asking if people are "just looking," you're allowing them to have that mindset. Your goal should be to have them develop an ownership mentality. They have a need to be fulfilled and are conducting research to find the right person or company to serve them.

> Thanks for coming in today. Let me ask you, are you candidates for new furniture today, or are you just researching **your options?**

Have to

As a salesperson, never make your customers feel as though you are there because you *have* to be. They'll feel better (and less pressured) knowing that you are *happy* to be there serving them.

> I'll have to go see if we have any in stock. Hang on while I call the warehouse.

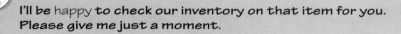

> I'll be happy to check our inventory on that item for you. Please give me just a moment.

Prospects

Although the word *prospects* has been a favorite for a long time, today it's more appropriate to refer to prospects as *future clients*. Referring to the prospects as future clients is a form of assumptive closing that, when used properly (and with sincerity), demonstrates your confidence in your ability to meet the clients' needs and become their new supplier.

> I hear from your friend that you're a prospect for my services.

CHAMPION STRATEGY #1

As a future client, do you have any questions for me? I'd also like to take this opportunity to ask you a few questions and take some notes on your responses so I can help you determine exactly what you require in this product.

Practice makes perfect: Pop quiz

Because repetition is the mother of learning, take a few moments to fill in the blanks using your new positive image words. Pay careful attention!

1. I don't handle objections. I'm going to take care of any _____ you may be having.

2. Our product isn't cheaper than our competition. The people who have purchased the product find that it is _____ .

3. I'd like to go over the figures with you to ensure that they make sense. We'll have more privacy in the _____ .

4. They aren't our customers; they are who we _____ .

5. Don't ever call those who are just looking lookers. They are _____ the product.

6. I don't have to serve you; rather I'm _____ to be here helping you.

7. I don't call my people prospects; rather, they are _____ .

Answer key:

1. Concerns

2. More economical

3. Conference room

4. Serve

5. Researching

6. Happy

7. Future clients

Overcoming Fear in General

Identifying the customer's fear isn't always easy. When figuring out exactly what the customer's afraid of is as easy as pulling an elephant through a keyhole, you have to take several steps to get the customer to voice his fears.

Start out by putting yourself in the customer's place. Ask yourself what you would want a salesperson to do with you (with you as the client) in the same situation. Act on whatever comes to mind. Continue to do this throughout the close as it will help you address the customer's fears and concerns. If you would be feeling a certain way in the same situation, chances are that the customer's feeling it right now.

The next thing you need to do is empower the customer by putting him in control of the questioning process by saying:

> What questions do you have regarding this product and how it meets your needs?

Also, before you ask the customer any question that can possibly create fear, reveal something about yourself that helps the customer relate to you. People are empowered when they believe they're not alone in a situation. Be the good guy — be on their side.

> You know, when I'm not here at work, I'm a consumer just like you. What I hope to find when I have a buying decision to make is someone with excellent product knowledge who can answer all of my questions. My job here, today, is to be the expert you rely on for information. So, please share with me your questions and concerns regarding this product and let's see how I can help you.

WARNING!

Overcoming your fear of their fear

Instead of doing all the things that help customers set aside their fears, many salespeople are unable to face their own fears of rejection, so they avoid dealing with the fear factor altogether. After all, they're trying to persuade someone they've never met before to part with his or her hard-earned money for their product or service. The salesperson has no idea going in what the customers' personality type is, what their financial situation is, or what their hopes and expectations are for the product. These fearful salespeople have no idea how the customers will react, so they decide to ignore the customer's fear, hoping that it will just go away. Well, it won't. You have to address the customer's fear. No customer is going to make a buying decision when they're scared.

On the other hand, some salespeople try so hard to relate to the customer that they sympathize themselves right out of a sale. You don't have to become the customer and experience all his problems; you just have to understand how the customer feels and then help him turn those fearful emotions into buying emotions.

Some salespeople become so impatient with customers who can't make a decision that instead of putting the customers at ease, they either show their true colors and adopt an uncaring attitude, or they give up the sale and let the customer know they're ready to move on to the next available customer. I've actually heard salespeople do just this. They say things like, "Well, let me know if I can be of any more assistance," or, "Call me when you make up your mind." Then they rush off before the customers can actually ask for more advice or answers.

What's sad for these salespeople is that instead of closing potentially great customers, they give up trying to close them and let the customer off the hook — maybe just about the time the customers were ready to say yes. So what happens? The customers go elsewhere. And when the customers enter the next selling situation, many of their questions have been answered and their minds are made up. Because of you, the new salesperson is able to close them in a flash. You don't even get a thank you for the warm-up!

Overcoming Fear in Particular

Refuse to accept fear as a reason your customers decide not to own your product or service. Remove fear from the equation by creating comfort in place of fear. How? Get active when you see fear creep in. Distract the customers from their fears. Make them remember instances when they said yes and everything turned out great. Identify the source of the fear and do what you can to bring it out into the open. Fear is always much more powerful when lurking just below the surface, stalking the customers who are ready to own. Help the customers face their fear and diminish its power.

So, how do you do all of this? You keep asking questions. The deeper the fear, the more questions you must ask to uncover it. When you've done a great job at getting rid of the fear, go for the final close. Use the following closes to turn the tables on Mr. Fear. Each close is designed to overcome fear and bring you and your customers to a successful end.

Understanding the decision-making process

Decisions are made emotionally. Not only are purchasing decisions made when buyers are in an emotional state, the decision is also linked emotionally to feelings about the salesperson and the product or service. This is where you, the salesperson, need to show up as the white knight on your valiant steed to defeat wily Mr. Fear. When you accomplish this feat, you empower the customer by making him feel confident in his wise decision to own, and the customer links good feelings about himself with you and your product.

If during the decision-making process something very negative happens, your customers may link negativity to you and your product. For instance, say they decided to own your product, but then they overhear a conversation between another representative and an unhappy customer. What do you think they will picture when they think of you? Dissatisfied customers. This is a bad link — perhaps an inaccurate link — but a link all the same. If you know this has happened, explain to the future client how you would personally handle that situation.

Much of the decision-making process is also based on previous decisions the customers made and the results of those decisions. If they previously owned a minivan that was something of a lemon, they're going to have some past prejudices, which you have to recognize and overcome. Past prejudices can apply to any product or service they've previously owned.

You need to clear the customers' minds and wipe the slate clean of any misconceptions about your product or service. Differentiate yourself and your product from the negative experiences of the past. I know salespeople who go so far as to walk in with a white board and markers and list the previous challenges and concerns that the client had. As the salesperson discusses how much better her company handles those areas of concern, the salesperson has the prospective new client erase each challenge on the list. Here's some of the phraseology to use:

> The way that challenge should have been handled is this. . . .

and then say:

> Do you agree that it would have made you happier that way?

When they agree, say:

> That's how we at Acme Everything handle that type of situation. In fact, I have the names of other clients you can ask about this particular situation if you'd like.

When they're confident and feel comfortable with you and your product, have them erase their concern right off the board. And you end up with a literally clean slate.

You may need to focus on yourself rather than your product. If the customers are comparing products that are very similar and they cannot distinguish the difference, concentrate on distinguishing between your salesmanship and that of your competitor. Reinforce and boost the level of confidence they feel in you personally. Show them that you'll serve their needs better than the other guy or gal. Then, make sure you live up to the belief they put in your ability to serve them.

The "If you say yes" close

In this close, you begin the closing statement with "If you say yes. . ." and complete the statement with something that gives the customer incredible benefits. For example:

> If you say yes to what I'm proposing here today, you'll have financial freedom for the rest of your life.

or

> If you say yes, you'll have the satisfaction of knowing your son will have the financial resources to complete his college education and walk across the stage on graduation day.

By using the "If you say yes" close, you definitely turn the tables on Mr. Fear. If fear tells the potential client to say no, the client is forced to think of what *won't* happen if he says no. So the fear becomes that the son won't be able to graduate from college or that there will be no financial freedom. This strategy makes the client reevaluate the situation — and he's more apt to say yes to you.

The negative economy close

During your sales career, you're bound to encounter at least one negative economy situation that requires the negative economy close. And even if the economy isn't really all that bad, you'll meet up with a Joe and Jennie Negative who firmly believe that the economy is bad in their little section of the world. When you encounter Mr. Fear in these situations, here's what you say:

> Years ago I learned a truth. Successful people buy when everyone else is selling and sell when everyone else is buying. There are many people talking about the bad economy these days, and I've decided not to let it bother me. Do you know why? Because many of today's fortunes were built during poor economic times. The people who built these fortunes saw the long-term opportunity rather than the short-term challenges. They made buying decisions and became successful. Of course, they had to be willing to make positive decisions. You have the same opportunity to make the same kind of decision today.

The facts presented in this sample dialogue are true. If you studied the major companies of today, you would see that most of them began when everyone else was immobilized — they took advantage of the opportunity. The negative economy close is a very true, beautiful close. The beauty of it is that after hearing this, the customers realize that going with Mr. Fear may hold them back from growing their business, achieving greatness, and beating the competition.

The big bargain close

Everyone is always looking for a bargain. However, the bargain is in the eye of the beholder. If your client has expressed a concern regarding rising prices, you're working with someone who fears inflation. Help this client view your offering as a bargain.

> During inflation, everything is a bargain. Do you know why? During inflation, knowledgeable people exchange money for things. During a deflation, they exchange things for money. So following this reasoning, whatever you acquire today will be more expensive tomorrow. This (name your product or service) is a bargain today because inflation may hit pricing tomorrow, and you do want a bargain, don't you?

The big bargain close doesn't work with high-tech equipment. The equipment is quickly outdated and the new releases are more and more economical. With high-tech products, you have to sell the strong value of having immediate benefits and stress that those benefits will save them money in the long run. Get the customers to understand how much productivity they can lose (in dollars, if you must) should they decide to wait for prices to come down. So remember to modify the big bargain close when dealing with high-tech products.

The money or nothing close

The money or nothing close works great for long-term purchases like homes, furniture, a special vacation, and so on. You can also use it with education products like a seminar on selling skills. The point of the close is to increase the value of the products that you're offering above the value of holding onto money.

You know, everything depreciates — cars, homes, retirement plans, products, even money itself. These days, all of us have to make the same decisions. Do we want to retain all of our spendable income and watch it depreciate? Or do we want to invest some of it on things we really want, things that will provide enjoyment for our families and ourselves? By the way, I wouldn't want you to make this decision if I wasn't so sure, but from what you've told me, you would receive the benefits from my product for years to come.

Again, sincerity is critical here. You must truly believe and express this belief in the joy, additional income, or satisfaction your product will provide the client.

Increase productivity close

Oftentimes when marketing to clients of a corporation, they aren't aware of how much an increase in morale can add to the productivity of the entire company. The business or productivity close brings that point home, so you're not only educating your clients on the power of employee morale, but giving them something to prove it with. This close pours on value for the benefits of your product.

What I'm offering is not just a good health insurance program; it's a boost in employee morale. Have you ever noticed how anything new increases job interest and excitement? Excitement increases morale. Morale increases productivity, and what is increased productivity worth?

Increased productivity is worth a heck of a lot to any company. Point out to your clients that increased productivity can generate enough increased income to more than make up for the increased investment. On top of that, point out to the clients how investing in your product can also increase loyalty and reduce turnover, thus saving them even more money on advertising for new hires. Wow, all that from a four-sentence close!

The competitive edge close

Everyone wants to be the best. They want market share. Companies need ways to increase their competitive edge. The competitive edge close appeals to the desire in the buyer to get ahead of the competition.

> Realize that many of your competitors are facing the same challenges as you are. Isn't it interesting that when an entire industry is fighting the same forces, some companies do a better job of meeting those challenges than others? My entire objective here today has been to provide you with a method of getting a competitive edge. And gaining edges, large or small, is how you can make your company one of those few companies in your industry that is doing a better job.

Fear would have kept the client's company from doing a better job — it would have kept them from implementing what you have to offer, which gives them that leg up on the competition. With this close, you've greatly diminished the power of fear by instilling a fear of what will happen if they *don't* go ahead.

The law of 10 close

The law of 10 close operates under the assumption that everyone has had at least one experience in their lives for which they have to admit that they're ten times better off because of the experience. This close works exceptionally well with things that build memories like cameras, vacations, and holiday events. This close also works for computers, time saving devices, and security devices. After all, one instance of a smoke alarm saving someone's life or a prized possession makes the investment appear minuscule, doesn't it?

> I've found over the years that a good test of the value of something is to determine whether or not it will stand the test of ten times. For example, you may have invested in a home, car, clothes, jewelry, or something that gave you great pleasure. But after you owned the item for awhile, how would you answer this question: "Am I willing now to pay ten times more for this product than I originally did?"

(continued)

(continued)

> In other words, has the product given you that much pleasure? If you paid for some advice that greatly improved your health, it was worth more than you paid for it. If you received some information that allowed you to have a life-changing experience or increase your income or self-image, it was worth more than you paid for it. There are a lot of things in our lives that I think we would have paid ten times more for them, considering what they've done for us.
>
> Now, step with me into the future. Ten years from now, will today's investment be worth more or less to you than what you're investing in it today?

If your product or service fits the category just described, this is a great close, because it takes the client away from the immediate financial decision and helps them to focus on the overall benefits and future rewards. The law of 10 close is excellent for diffusing money concerns.

The make it better close

The make it better close can be used when customers tell you that they've done business with salespeople in the past who didn't call back and didn't give them good service, and they're afraid the same thing will happen with you. An important thing to remember is that you never knock your competition — knocking others makes you look small and petty.

> First of all, even though it wasn't my company, I apologize for times other companies have sold you products and then let you down with the follow-up and service. Let me assure you, our company will always be available to you and will contact you on a scheduled basis to make sure of your satisfaction. In fact, that's one of the reasons I chose to work with this company. We are always here for our customers. Your ongoing business is important to us, and I won't do anything to jeopardize the relationship we're establishing here today.

For the times when the poor salesperson *is* from your company, take a look at this chapter's section "Your buyer's fear is based on bad past experiences" for how to handle the situation.

The buyer's remorse close

I'm sure you're all familiar with *buyer's remorse* — briefly, it's when a client has second thoughts about the decision he's made to purchase your product and he takes advantage of the opportunity to cancel the transaction. (To find out more about buyer's remorse, see Chapter 10.) Buyer's remorse is a favorite of Mr. Fear's. Buyer's remorse raises doubts about the decision. It builds regret. And it's a master of instigating second-guessing. Use the buyer's remorse close to take some of the wind out of Mr. Fear's sails — or is it sales? (Sorry, the pun was too good to pass up.)

I feel good about the decision you've made to get involved in this insurance program. I can tell that you're both excited and somewhat relieved. From time to time, I've had people just like you who were positive about the decision they'd made until they shared it with a friend or relative. Well-meaning friends or relatives, not understanding all the facts and maybe even a little envious, discouraged them from their decision for one reason or another. Please don't let this happen to you. In fact, if you think you may change your mind, please tell me now.

By asking the customers to tell you now if they're a little dubious, you can take the opportunity to resell value and recap the benefits of owning your product. Use this close and you'll reduce the number of lost sales caused by buyer's remorse.

The economic truth close

When your product is of higher quality and a little less economical than the competition's, use the economic close to instill doubt about the other product and value in yours:

Guiding your buying decision by price alone is not always wise. Investing too much is never recommended; however, investing too little has its drawbacks as well. By spending too much, you lose a little money, but that's all. By spending too little, you risk more because the item you've purchased may not give you the satisfaction you were expecting. That it's seldom possible to get the most by spending the least is an economic truth.

(continued)

(continued)

> In considering business with the least expensive supplier, it may be wise to add a little to your investment to cover the risk you're taking in purchasing a lesser product. If you agree with me on this point and are willing and able to invest a little more, why not get a superior product? After all, the inconveniences of an inferior product are difficult to forget. When you receive the benefits and satisfaction from the superior product, its price, no matter how much, will soon be forgotten, don't you agree?

Now you're making Mr. Fear work with you. Fear may have initially made the customer not want to spend too much. But with this close, the customer will begin to fear making a bad decision and losing face by buying an inferior product. Your argument for investing a little more may first cause confusion on the part of the customer, but then the answer becomes perfectly clear: buy your superior product and avoid any risks of an inferior one.

The time trap close

The time trap close is kind of long, but it's extremely valuable for certain products like insurance and investments because it demonstrates how quickly things can pass us by. If we don't pay attention and take care of things now, we may have regrets later. The logic behind this close is incredible and it builds emotionally as you go through it.

You:	Over 90 percent of the people in the United States won't have the kind of money they need to retire comfortably during their golden years. The biggest reason for this, I feel, is what I call the time trap. To illustrate this point, I'm going to ask you a question. What do you feel you'll be doing 25 years from now?
Them:	Well, that's so far in the future, but hopefully we'll be retired and enjoying ourselves.
You:	Yes, I hope you will be, too, but it will take more than hope. We need to turn that hope into reality. Try to imagine life 25 years from now.

What will the world be like? I know it seems incredibly far away, but is it really that far in the future? Let's look at 25 years in a different light. What were you doing 25 years ago?

Them: Let's see, uh, we were in high school.

You: When you look back at high school, can you remember your senior prom and some of the things you were doing in high school?

Them: Yes.

You: Does it look very far away?

Them: No, it seems like just yesterday.

You: That yesterday was 25 years ago. Isn't it amazing? If you were sitting in high school discussing what you would be doing now, 25 years later, it would have seemed really far away , but when you look back at it, high school seems like just yesterday. Time passing too quickly is the situation millions of older Americans are finding themselves in now. Back 25 years ago, when you were in high school, these older folks were 40 years old but still thought that today was too far away and wasn't worth considering. Now, 25 years later, they're working two part-time jobs just to make their Social Security checks stretch far enough to eat and keep a roof over their heads. Time has a way of looking like a wide expanse into the future, yet it compresses as we look back into the past. I want to make sure that 25 years from now, you're not looking back and wondering where the time went with no time left to enjoy your golden years. I'm here to help you avoid the terrible ramifications of this time trap that's trapping over 90 percent of the people in this country. Now, let's see what we can do about securing your financial future.

Pretty good, huh? You've taken your clients from the carefree days of high school to the potentially care-burdened days of retirement in a matter of minutes. No one wants to picture themselves flipping burgers at 65 like they did at 16. Back then, it may have been fun. Now it may not be.

Be sure you know the personality type of the client before attempting this close. The thought of flipping burgers at 65 may make Mr. Smith feel like a kid again, and he may want something like this to occupy his time.

The gaining versus losing close

You will come across clients who are more afraid of not having the benefits of the new product, which is a negative motivation, than they are excited about having them — a positive motivation. For example, this fear may occur with a piece of manufacturing equipment that will put the client on the cutting edge and ahead of the competition. The fear that the competition will outpace the client may be the biggest motivation to own.

You may also find this type of fear in families where there's a lot of competition and they're always trying to outdo each other by having the smallest portable telephone, the biggest big-screen TV, or the newest model of car or computer. In those cases, you need to build the emotional appeal and commitment to the product or service based on those facts. If you hear any hesitancy, you can subtly remind them that this is the latest and greatest item on earth and that they'll be the first in the neighborhood, maybe even in town, to have one — but only if that's the truth, of course. Nobody likes to miss out on the good things in life, so make the customer feel like they'll be missing out on all kinds of things if they decide not to own.

Without asking the customer some questions, you won't be able to tell which is their strongest motivator — the negative or the positive. You have to discover some important information. For example:

  ✔ How long have they been looking for your product or service? If it's been a long time and they still haven't been closed, they are probably not very motivated by the pain of not owning your offering.

  ✔ Ask them how they've been getting along without owning a product like the one you offer. If they tell you how miserable it has been and complain about the discomfort of not owning, you can probably rest assured that they are motivated by the pain of not owning your product.

✔ Ask them how owning your product will make them feel. For example:

> Gee, what's it going to feel like to drive out of here in that brand new Lincoln?

If the customers start talking about their excitement of driving across country in their new car and showing it off to their relatives, you can assume they're motivated by the fun and excitement of ownership instead of the pain of not owning.

After you discover what motivates the customers, close them accordingly. You can keep the sale closed by continuing to point out the pain of not owning or the pleasure of owning, depending on what pushes their *hot buttons* — benefits they've indicated that they want to own.

Adapting to the Emotional Environment

The more you study human emotions, the more you realize how we all communicate our feelings quite differently. To handle the differing ways people express themselves, you have to be a chameleon. A chameleon has the ability to change to the environment, to blend. Emotionally, this is what you have to do as a professional salesperson — you need to blend with each situation. As a master closer, you must not only be emotionally flexible to change, but also you have to form a comfortable fit in communicating with your customers to put them at ease. You must be willing to adapt, to relate to them. Being able to blend like this will take work. You have to stop talking and expressing values, be willing to ask questions, listen, and then respond to customers in a way to which they are most able to relate. If all you're aiming for is average sales with average ability to close, you can continue your current practices. To be a master, however, you've got to be versatile.

Chapter 7

Putting an End to Procrastination

In This Chapter

▶ Defining procrastination

▶ Figuring out why people procrastinate

▶ Understanding tricks customers use to procrastinate

▶ Exploring closes that end procrastination

*P*rocrastination can wreak more havoc on business productivity than Godzilla in Tokyo. Procrastination is easy to identify when it's a flagrant disregard for getting work done and for getting decisions made. Recognizing procrastination is one thing; doing something about it is another. In this chapter, I cover both areas (recognition and doing something about it) and also show you how to become more effective when dealing with procrastination.

Procrastination Defined

My own personal definition of procrastination is this: Living yesterday, avoiding today, thus ruining tomorrow. If you avoid making decisions today, you're setting the stage for tomorrow not to be a better day, but to be just like today. When today becomes yesterday and the days are the same because you haven't changed, haven't made any decisions, haven't kept up, you're living in the past because everyone and everything else in the world will pass you by. No one will stop and wait because it's not convenient for you to keep up just now.

On the other hand, when you're dealing with a procrastinating customer, it's up to you to either stop and wait for the customer to make decisions or figure out a way to get the customer moving toward owning your product or service. I go over many of the ways to move things along in this chapter.

 Living in the past is not acceptable in today's fast-paced global marketplace. Just think, a few years ago, you were out of touch if you didn't have a dedicated fax line. Today, an e-mail address is vital to your business.

If you're just keeping up, you'll never get ahead. Your goal with your products and services should be to help your clients live better, make or save more money, and stay at least a couple steps ahead of their competition. In today's world, this is sometimes a big order to fill because the competition is moving ahead every day, too. You have to stay on your toes to make it.

For some people, just thinking about keeping up — not actually doing it — is so overwhelming that they do nothing. Procrastination takes over. The trouble with procrastinators is that they can make it look like they're getting a lot accomplished when they're really just treading water. They refuse to make a decision because they need more information, but they're so busy making themselves *look* busy that they never actually get around to making a decision. So when the time comes and the decision must be made, the procrastinator tends to drown in a sea of panic. The trick for you, the sales professional who's trying to close a procrastinator, is to invite him into your lifeboat and save his skin in a hurry.

Why Do Customers Procrastinate?

The reasons why people procrastinate can be any number of things. In order to choose the best method for helping customers get over their current bout of procrastination, you have to find out what their particular reason is. The most common reasons are listed in the following sections.

Whatever the fear is that may be holding the customers back, realize that it's not your fault. Unless you were the salesperson who helped them acquire something they later regretted, you're not the bad guy or gal. So don't take their hesitation personally. You do, however, get to be the hero in helping them overcome their procrastination and move on to enjoying the benefits of your product or service.

Fear of making decisions

If your client is fearful of making decisions, you need to be patient and ask a lot of questions. Get the customers talking about why they're hesitant and listen for something solid you can grab hold of and help them with.

A common fear of the customer is making a bad decision. Maybe the customer made a poor decision in the past on a similar purchase and is afraid it will happen again. You have to clearly show the customer that this is an entirely different situation with different products and (hopefully) even more benefits than the past situation held for them.

(For more information on overcoming a customer's fear, take a look at Chapter 6.)

Lack of trust in you

Maybe the customer has been told over and over again to never trust a salesperson. Believe me, there are millions of people out there who think like this. Unfortunately, there's also a large number of untrustworthy salespeople in the world who perpetuate the belief that salespeople can't be trusted. You, however, are different. You are a sales *professional*. You can be trusted to help your clients meet their needs and make decisions that are truly good for them. You just need to help them see this so they'll go ahead and listen to your recommendations. Prove this by doing the following:

- ✔ Pay attention.

- ✔ Provide the utmost in courtesy.

   Hold doors open for clients. Say "thank you" and "you're welcome."

- ✔ Lead them to the product of interest all the while asking about their needs.

- ✔ Respect their time.

   If you know your product demonstration takes only 10 minutes, promise them you won't take more than 12 minutes of their time. Some salespeople I know even put their watches or a stopwatch in plain sight of the client and are certain to wrap up their demonstration in less than the promised time. They make a point of showing the client how they valued their time by not running over.

- ✔ Fulfill your promises and deliver on time.

Wanting your attention

Ever consider the thought that maybe the customers enjoy your attention and don't want the process to end? Hey, you're a nice person to be around, right? If you sense that your easy rapport with your customers is part of what they're buying (as it should be), take a few moments to let them know that they're not just investing in a product or service; they're establishing a long-term relationship with you and your company. Now's the time to tell the customers about your follow-up program. If you give some sort of recognition for referred leads who also become clients, tell them about that program as well. Make your customers feel like they're not just getting a product — they're joining the family of happy clients your company serves. Affiliating the customer with your "family" may be just the ticket for getting the customers to make their decision now.

Seeking education

The customer may balk and say that he doesn't know enough about the product to make a decision. If you feel you've done a good job of getting the information across and the customers still hesitate, do a brief summary of all the points you've covered. Ask what you may have missed. You should be able to do this quickly from the extensive notes you've taken during your time with this client. Better yet, you should have a summary page in your proposal that provides just that information.

Here is one case of procrastination that may be your fault. You may not have been thorough enough in your presentation, leaving the client feeling that he doesn't know enough to make an educated decision. Strive to cover every aspect of your product in an effort to make the customer comfortable. You can't call yourself a sales professional if you don't have the skills to discover the most important needs of each client and educate him or her on the features and benefits of the product you represent.

Comparing apples to oranges

If your product is being compared to that of the competition, you need to ask a lot of questions about how the competition presented their information. You need to be certain that both products are considered on the same basis. While it may seem indiscreet to ask what the competition is offering (when, for example, the client is asking you to bid against a competitor), it's never inappropriate to ask how the information is presented. You do it this way:

> **You:** Your complete and total satisfaction is our goal. I want you to have the best product for your specific needs and would never recommend something if I didn't truly believe it was in your best interest. I'm certain you're taking great pains in analyzing our product against that of the competition. I'm curious, though, about the analysis itself. Are you finding that our information has been provided in a format similar to that of the other company?

The customer may come back with something like:

> **Them:** Well, it's a bit different, so I'm having to convert some of the figures to get to the same bottom line.

Never let the clients do the conversions themselves. One minor math error on their part can mean an end to the biggest sale of your career. *Always* revise your data to meet their needs.

Now that you know that finding the same bottom line is a bit of a challenge in the decision-making process, ask for the details. Get on your computer and revise your numbers so you can deliver the figures in the same way the competition did. Your extra efforts will show your determination to do well in serving their needs and may also help the customer make his decision much more quickly — hopefully in your favor.

Lack of interest in the product

Sometimes your potential clients may not seem to care too much about your product or service, so they procrastinate making a decision either way. When this happens, you need to be prepared to build value. Show the customers what's in it for them. As an example, say you're talking to a parent about the latest video game. They may never play it, so they have rather lukewarm feelings about it. To make a close, you're going to have to build the value of the child's appreciation into your sale of the game. Using this approach will be more effective than talking about how you can blast 500 aliens into smithereens in three minutes.

> Just picture the delight and excitement on your son's face when he opens this gift on Christmas morning. He'll know you cared enough to get him just what he wanted.

If they've made any disparaging remarks about little Johnny during your time with them, you can add:

> Plus, he'll run off to the den to play it for at least two hours, giving you some time to relax.

Always remember: The benefit of the product is in the eye of the buyer. Your job is to determine which approach to use and then deliver accordingly.

Signs of a Procrastination in Progress

Certain traits are common among procrastinators. If you're beginning to suspect that your customer is a procrastinator, here are some things to watch for. If you see any of the following signs, your suspicions are probably correct.

Changing the subject

Procrastinators will talk to you about almost anything except the situation at hand, which — in this case — is making a buying decision. You'll know more about their kids, their golf game, their last vacation, their hobbies, even the personality conflicts in their offices than you will about their buying preferences. If you encounter customers like this, be patient. Learn to listen well. Watch for an opportunity to redirect the conversation back to the purchase. Ask them a question that brings them back to the subject at hand. The customers may counter by asking you questions about yourself, your kids, the car you drive, etc. Everything they counter with is a stall. Your mission is to keep dragging them back to the selling situation with questions regarding their needs. You may have to pointedly ask what exactly is going on if the chitchat drags on too long or the customers change the subject every time you take control:

> You: I sense that you're not really ready to make a decision on this product today.
>
> Them: Well, I really haven't made up my mind yet on what I'm going to do.
>
> You: That's no problem. Can you tell me what your thoughts are so far so I can tell if there may be some information I've left out of my presentation?

Let the customers summarize their thinking. Take note of not just what they say, but how they say it. Try to discern the area of discomfort and then review the details.

If the meeting gets a bit drawn out and you don't feel there's anything you can do to make the sale today, reschedule.

I can tell you're not really ready to go ahead and that you may just need a bit more time to consider this purchase. Why don't we schedule another meeting for Thursday morning when we're both fresh and you can give the matter your full attention?

Rescheduling is a last resort tactic. If you're in the game against the competition, it may be to your advantage to risk going for the close today rather than having the competition spend more time with the client. However, if you truly feel you're getting nowhere, move onto other clients and reschedule your time with this one.

Making a move: Body language

People tend to make several body language moves when they want to slow things down. By watching their body language, you can generally target a procrastinator right off the bat. The following lists several moves procrastinators tend to make:

- ✔ Taking off their glasses to clean the lenses and/or chewing on the ear piece
- ✔ Pushing backward in a chair
- ✔ Tapping a pen or playing with a paper clip
- ✔ Glancing out the window
- ✔ Shuffling papers or flipping the pages of your proposal

Any of these signs tell you that the customers aren't really ready to go ahead with a decision. Now your job is to find out why:

- ✔ Did you just say something prior to one of these moves that may have raised a concern? If so, restate that point and ask if it's something you need to clarify.
- ✔ Did the buyers just think of a detail that had been left out of previous conversations? If so, they may be a bit embarrassed to bring it up now. You can solve this by asking:

How are you feeling about all of this so far? Are we covering all the details you're concerned about?

✔ Do the customers simply feel you're moving too fast?

> I know it may seem that we're moving along quite rapidly; however, you seem to be grasping the information quite well. What questions do you have at this point?

✔ Maybe the customers see no further reason to hold off making the purchase but are allowing themselves time to second-guess.

> I sense some hesitation on your part. Can you elaborate on the reasons why you may not go ahead with this decision?

I can't state strongly enough the value and the power of learning to read body language. If you're truly serious about your career in selling, being able to read a person through body language can save you a lot of time and grief, and most importantly, can help you serve your clients better than the average bear. (For more on reading body language, see Chapter 2.)

Allowing interruptions

Say you're dealing with Joe Customer. Joe is handling the negotiations of a purchase of computer equipment for a new branch office his company is opening. Obviously, you can expect things to be hectic. Joe agrees to meet with you and when you arrive, you notice that he doesn't close his office door when you enter. Uh-oh. An open door is an open invitation for interruptions. Then Joe sits behind his desk with several stacks of papers between the two of you — another potential source of distraction. The phone rings and Joe makes a face as if to say "This will just take a minute." He then takes the call, handling a matter totally unrelated to your computer equipment. Is Joe serious about making a decision, or is he procrastinating? More then likely he's procrastinating. However, he may not even be fully aware of what he's doing.

With the Joe Customers of the world, I recommend that you subtly take control. Upon entering the room, simply close the door. Chances are, the customer won't even immediately register the fact that the door is closed. If your closing the door appears to concern the customer, say:

> Do you mind if I close this? I'd hate to have anything distract us from something so critical as the purchase of a new product.

With regard to the desk, suggest you sit at a conference table if the customer has one. If not, say:

> I have a few things to show you and will need a bit of space. Can I help you clear some of these things out of the way?

Finally, add:

> Just one more thing. Do you have a secretary who can screen your calls for our brief time together?

or:

> Do you have a Do Not Disturb feature on your phone that we could take advantage of? I understand how valuable your time is, and I don't want to take up any more of it than necessary today, so the fewer interruptions the better, don't you agree?

By eliminating the distractions, you diminish the chances of procrastination taking over your closing sequence. Being proactive is critical when it comes to facing down procrastination.

Canceling Visits

The selling business is rife with canceled appointments. Buyers cancel visits ten minutes after you confirm them. They cancel the night before via voice mail so they don't risk talking with you in person. They cancel by calling you on your cellular phone as you're driving to their office. Sometimes, they even have the receptionist tell you they've canceled after you've arrived on time, fully prepared and ready to close.

Now, there will be times when something truly important comes up and there's a legitimate reason for the cancellation. In most of these cases, the client is happy to reschedule with you — and will go out of his way to be prepared for the next time. After all, he sort of owes you, right?

However, you're bound to encounter procrastinators who put off seeing you like they put off a visit to the dentist for a root canal. Here's how to handle someone you sense will put off your next scheduled visit. First of all, when the time is set, immediately put a confirmation in writing. Send the confirmation via fax, e-mail, or regular mail (if the next visit is a few days away).

Call to confirm your appointment at the end of the preceding day if you're scheduled to visit in the morning. If you have an afternoon appointment, confirm the morning of the same day. Here's what to say when you call to confirm:

Hi, this is (your name here). I'm really looking forward to our time together at (confirm again the time, date, and location). I really put some work into the presentation and pulled together some exciting information that you're going to be surprised to hear about this product. The time with me will be time well spent, I promise you that. I'll see you then.

Now, if you deliver these lines with sincerity and enthusiasm, how can the customer cancel on you? You've worked so hard for him! Also, you've built his curiosity about the "exciting information" you have in store for him. After this, if the customer does feel the urge to cancel an appointment, it won't be with you.

By the way, top salespeople — especially those who work with consumers — refer to appointments as *visits,* a kinder, gentler term that doesn't raise barriers of fear.

Not returning calls

Procrastinators are excellent at shuffling messages, losing messages, misplacing phone numbers, and letting time slip away from them — so they just *couldn't* get back to you.

If you know you're working with a procrastinator who uses this method, try not to leave the ball in his court. Leave assumptive messages like:

> If I don't hear from you otherwise, I'll assume the higher-end model is the one you're most interested in. I'll have the demo delivered by tomorrow afternoon.

Now, if the client isn't interested in that model, chances are pretty good that you'll hear from him. Plus, having a demo model show up and having other staff people ooh and ahh over it only to have to return the product makes the buyer look a bit incompetent.

One of my students handles voice mail with procrastinators this way: He identifies himself and leaves his number at the beginning of the message, and then halfway through an enticing sentence or question, he cuts off the call. Some people may think this tactic is a bit slick or theatrical. Well, this method won't work in all cases, but it does in some. If you do try this and it works, remember to use it only once with each client. This student of mine says that he uses this as a last resort with clients he knows he can serve but who won't return his calls.

A little understanding goes a long way. You may have a client who is quite simply overwhelmed with his current work load and returning calls to salespeople gets shoved to the bottom of his priority list. In cases like this, just be persistent and sympathetic. Give him a call for action and a deadline for recontacting you about a critical element. A deadline may be what gets you moved up on the priority list.

> I understand that you're extremely busy right now and want to let you know that I'm still here to meet your data processing needs when you're ready to discuss them. In our last conversation, you were considering adding three new ports. I wanted to get back with you to let you know that we can schedule that installation as soon as Friday of this week if you'll get back with me by Wednesday at 10:00 a.m. If you can't break away long enough to call me, feel free to have someone else in your organization relay the message and I'll handle everything from that point on.

Offering an alternate suggestion for communication is also a good idea. Some people respond better to e-mail than to voice mail because they can do it on their own time, not during set business hours.

Wanting to do lunch — a long lunch

Some potential clients will take advantage of you by dangling their business out there in front of you, and then subtly or not so subtly suggesting that you discuss your proposal with them over lunch, at an NBA or NFL game, on the golf course, and so on.

A lot of business is conducted outside the confines of homes and offices, and that's okay. You just need to be aware of who's serious about doing business with you and who's taking advantage. Polly Purchasing Agent, who can't seem to schedule you in for an appointment, but suggests meeting over lunch instead, may just be looking for a free lunch and not your products. You have to make judgment calls as to what you feel is best for each situation. If you do take Polly to lunch before she becomes a client, don't take her to the best restaurant in town — that would be inviting her to take advantage of you. If Polly dawdles over lunch and skirts around the business at hand, she's very likely a procrastinator and is using your lunch as a screen to cover for time she should be spending doing something else.

Handling Procrastinators with Ease

Procrastinators are comfortable just the way they are — they don't handle change well. The only way to get a procrastinator to make a move is to create so much desire for the outcome that they become uncomfortable staying the same and have to make the change to achieve a new level of comfort. The following sections discuss several ways to do just that.

Creating a sense of urgency

To get procrastinators off the fence, nothing works better than creating a sense of urgency. If you know there's a price increase for your product next month, use that knowledge to help your clients make decisions now that will save them money in the long run. Everyone wants to save money.

Another way to create a sense of urgency is with delivery dates:

> In order to make the January shipping date from manufacturing, I have to get your order in by the end of this week.

Working the guilt angle

For some procrastinators, guilt is what gets them moving. If they're uncomfortable about the current situation, but lack confidence in their own decision-making abilities, try using guilt.

Now I'm not advising you to try to push your customers into something. Only use the guilt angle when you know for certain that your product or service is truly good for your customers and that they can afford it.

For example, something most people — not just procrastinators — put off is saving for their childrens' educations or protecting themselves with enough insurance to have their families cared for if something should happen to them. No one is in a hurry to admit that before they know it, their children will be grown. No one wants to face the fact that they may not be around to see it happen. If you help procrastinating clients imagine a real life situation in which their own children are at risk, they'll most likely make an immediate move to become more comfortable regarding that situation. The way they get more comfortable is to increase their insurance coverage or start that mutual fund. Get them comfortable with the new sense of security this provides; then close the sale.

> The sooner you make this decision, the sooner your children will be financially protected should anything happen to you.

Showing customers how to be a hero

When your client is a decision maker — say a purchasing agent or business owner or head of household — he may make decisions about products or services that he will never personally use. In those cases, the decision maker may not be as motivated to make a decision (unless his staff or family is especially good at nagging). He isn't personally being restricted by not having cable television or the latest mailing equipment, so he doesn't feel the immediate reward, either.

In this case, you need to help that decision maker see himself as the hero who makes wise decisions that bring benefits to all those he cares about. Receiving gratitude or recognition for doing something good can be quite a motivator.

> I know you won't be the one using the new mail machine, but just imagine the delight of the staff when the new equipment makes the day pass faster and the job easier.

Assuming the close

Some people just don't want to make a decision because they have gotten used to bantering with you. They may not have other projects of interest to move on to. Or they may just not know how to wrap something up. When you're confident that you've covered all the bases and that not a single reason exists for the customers not to go ahead, you may have to get very assumptive and call for their approval on your paperwork.

> Because you have no further questions or concerns, I can assume that my company suits your needs. With your approval right here, I'll get your account established, and we'll be set up for business.

Having an agenda — in writing

Having an agenda works well with clients that you find yourself spending way too much time with. If you're with a new client, this strategy shows your dedication to staying on task and valuing their time. Simply go into your presentation with a brief agenda or checklist of the important items to cover. Then say the following:

> I so appreciate your time today. I know how busy you are. To keep us on track and keep our meeting as brief as possible, I've prepared a brief agenda of topics we'll need to cover.

Hand the agenda to the customer. Including check boxes on the agenda is helpful with some procrastinators as they can check off an item when you complete a topic. An agenda is a tool that enables you to keep the customers focused.

Don't put "Ask for the sale" on your list. Instead, you may want to word it this way: "Confirm that our product meets your needs."

Structure the agenda to call for the close as the second-to-last item. The last item should be to thank the customer for his business.

Recognizing the customer's stress

When customers procrastinate, they create a situation of constant worry. But isn't it better to just do what needs to be done when it needs to be done and with a clear head? Worry caused by procrastination can be a constant distraction; it can interrupt your days to the point that you're unproductive at everything. Help your clients get on with their other tasks by getting this decision made today.

> I understand that you're hesitant to make a decision today about my product. You probably have a lot on your mind. I learned a saying from a speaker once that makes a lot of sense when it comes to handling business matters. The saying goes like this: "I must do the most productive thing possible at every given moment." Makes sense, doesn't it? Now let me ask you, what's the most productive thing you could be doing right now?

If the customer says something that has little to do with the buying decision, say:

> Then, let's get this decision out of the way so you can get on to something more productive.

If the customer says the buying decision is the most productive thing he could be doing right now, say:

> Good. Then we're handling just what you want to do right now, which is to make a decision about my product. With your approval right here, we'll be in business.

Using the scale approach

The scale approach (see Figure 7-1) has been a decision-making tool for hundreds of years. I've refined and updated it for today's selling situations. In this strategy, I use a scale — something that's used to weigh various objects — to weigh the facts regarding the benefits of a product or service against the concerns that a client has about purchasing. When the client expresses hesitation or says that he wants to weigh it out in his mind, you, ever so kindly, offer to help.

> I understand how you feel, and weighing the facts before making a decision makes a lot of sense. In fact, when I'm in this type of situation, I use a method called the "Fact Weighing Scale Approach." Here's how it works: First, we draw a scale.

Figure 7-1: Scale illustration.

> On the left side of the scale, we pile up — just like small weights — the reasons you feel it makes good sense to go ahead with the purchase. On the right side of the scale, we pile up the reasons you feel are against the purchase. When we are finished, the decision will be weighed. Let's try it, okay?

Work with the customer to come up with reasons. Two tips when using this method: Go for a minimum of six reasons for the decision, and don't help on the right side!

> Let's see what we've got. On the left side of the scale, we have six heavy reasons why you should go ahead with the purchase. On the right side, we only have two against. So the answer seems apparent. Weighing the facts always makes things a little clearer, doesn't it?

Relating to a similar situation

Relating a story of someone else who was in a similar situation as the customer is always effective because the customer will identify with that person. Tell the customer about someone who procrastinated and wished he hadn't or conversely, someone who *didn't* procrastinate and received tremendous benefit from making an immediate buying decision.

> You know, about a month ago, I had a client facing a decision similar to the one you're considering today. He went ahead with our comprehensive medical plan and had a need to use it just last week. The situation was unfortunate; however, his burden would have been doubled had he not gone ahead with the insurance.

Thinking it over

You're guaranteed to hear a variation of the phrase "I want to think it over" from one out of every five new clients. Some of the variations you'll hear may be:

- "I want to sleep on it."
- "I'll get back to you."
- "We'll review all the facts, then make a decision."
- "We never make a decision on the first visit."

The exact words that are used matter little; what really matters is that you recognize the stall and are ready with this reply:

> That's fine. Obviously, you wouldn't take your time think-
> ing this purchase over unless you were seriously inter-
> ested. I mean, I'm sure you're not telling me that to get
> rid of me. So, may I assume you will give it very careful
> consideration?
>
> Just to clarify my thinking, what phase of this opportu-
> nity is it that you want to think over? Is it the quality of
> the service I'll render? Is it something I've forgotten to
> cover? Is it the return on your investment? Is it any of
> the financial aspects? Seriously, please level with me."

A tip when using this strategy: Don't pause after the word "over" —
if you do, a client is likely to answer "everything," or "the whole
idea of going ahead," and you're dead in the water. What you
want do here is review what they've already agreed to. In other
words, you're weeding out all the other objections and narrowing
it down to the most common final objection, which is the money.
Handle the money objection and begin reclosing.

Quoting General Colin Powell

General Powell made a statement during the Persian Gulf War
debriefings that riveted me. Using this quote from General Powell
can work wonders with a procrastinator.

> I recently heard about something that General Powell,
> one of the greatest military minds of our time, said. Here
> are his words: "Indecision has cost Americans, American
> business, and the American government billions of dol-
> lars. Far more than a wrong decision would have cost."
> What we're talking about now is a decision, isn't it? What
> will happen if you say yes and what will happen if you say
> no? If you say no, nothing will happen, and things will be
> the same tomorrow as they are today. If you say yes, . . .

Here you quickly go into three main benefits the customer gets
from owning your product, such as:

> You'll have financial freedom for the rest of your life, you'll have the satisfaction of watching your son walk across the stage on graduation day, and you'll be a part of a Fortune 100 company offering unlimited career opportunities.

Keeping track of inflation

The economy in the United States is a supply and demand economy, and we go through cycles of both inflation and deflation. I'm not sure exactly what the economical situation is in your area right now, but there are periods when I think this can be the most powerful close in your arsenal of techniques. Use this close when a person is dubious about the investment and they want to wait for things to come down, such as interest rates.

> The most critical decisions we have to make today are money decisions. We no longer have the luxury of deciding between three factors: save, spend, or invest. Today, because of inflation, we can no longer afford to just save our money, and I'm sure you know why: Every time Washington decides to keep rolling those money presses, every dollar we have saved is worth less than it was when we earned it. Today, we must make whatever money we have left after meeting our basic expenses do something positive for us. We really have only two choices: We can find an investment that will actually show a return greater than the inflation rate or we can improve our standard of living. Now, we have found what you really want. What you really deserve is a reward for all your hard work. Tell me, are you or are you not entitled to a reward for all the work you've done?

Showing that you get what you pay for

I know we've all heard it. The customer says "I can get it cheaper somewhere else" as a defense mechanism when often all the customer wants is time to shop. Using this closing technique will help the customer rationalize the decision and go ahead with your product today.

That you can find this product for less elsewhere may well be true, and in today's economy, we all want the most for our money. A truth that I have learned over the years is that the cheapest price is not always what we really want. Most people look for three things in making an investment: one, the finest quality; two, the best service, and three, the lowest price. I have never found a company that can offer all three — the finest quality and the best service at the lowest price. I'm curious. For your long-term happiness, which of the three are you willing to give up? Quality, service, or low price?

- ✔ Very few people are going to choose a low quality product. (Very few salespeople are going to want to represent one.)
- ✔ If the item being purchased requires a good bit of after-the-sale service such as computer equipment or cars, service won't be their choice. After all, who wants so-so service when you're without a car or your computer is down?
- ✔ The majority of people will choose low price because, after all, everyone knows the old cliché "you get what you pay for."

Fitting your product into the customer's budget

You often come across people who use their budget as a way to keep from committing to a purchase. Use this close to remind them of the true purpose of a budget and who's actually in control.

I understand your need to stick to your budget, which is why I contacted you in the first place. I'm fully aware of the fact that every well-managed business controls the flow of its money with a carefully planned budget. The budget is a necessary tool for every company to give direction to its goal. However, the tool itself doesn't dictate how the company is run. The budget must be flexible. You, as the controller of that budget, retain for yourself the right to flex that budget in the best interest of the company's financial present and competitive future, don't you? What we have been examining here today is a system which will allow your company an immediate and continuing competitive edge. Tell me, under these conditions, will your budget flex or will it dictate your actions?

This script can be tweaked for a personal sale, too, if people rely on their household budgets as the final stall. What they're really saying is that they don't see enough value to take the money from something else they've budgeted for and put it in your product.

I understand your need to stick to your budget. I'm fully aware of the need for people today to have a good handle on where their money goes. Would you agree with me that your budget is an excellent tool for helping you achieve the things you want with the money you earn? However, you are the one using the tool; the tool itself doesn't dictate how the money is spent. Your budget must be flexible for emergencies and changing needs, correct? You, as the controller of that budget, retain for yourself the right to flex that budget in your own best interest, don't you? What we have been examining here today is a product which will allow you (or your family) an immediate and continuing benefit. Tell me, under these conditions, will your budget flex or will it dictate your actions?

Having no regrets

Everyone has a regret or two regarding past decisions. This close assures the customers that this time, making the right decision today will eliminate any bad feelings in the future.

We're all members of the Wish I'da club: Wish I'da bought real estate in Arizona 15 years ago. Wish I'da bought stock years ago so I'd be rich today. Now, wouldn't it be great to get rid of at least one Wish I'da by saying yes to something you really want?

Reaching a compromise

Use this tactic when you have two or more decision makers who can't seem to agree on a decision. They both want the product and they're qualified for it, but they've come to an impasse and need a little nudge. They both know there are enough reasons why they should go ahead and make the decision today — you just need to help them along.

> When two people are required to make one decision, it's often impossible to find one solution that satisfies both of them. So life again becomes a matter of compromise. Now, the measurement of each decision is through the use of this question: Does the product satisfy most of the wants of each of the parties?

Incorporating a third party

In essence, the purpose of this close is to get permission to talk with a subordinate or third party when a decision maker is procrastinating. By giving authority to another, the decision maker is getting out of making the decision altogether and that's what some procrastinators want — not to be accountable.

> My experience in the past has proven that people in your position operate under terrific time constraints. I understand the value of your time. In many cases, my clients and I have both found it helpful for me to do most of my groundwork with someone you choose to give me the information I need to prepare a proposal for your fine company. Who is it that I should speak with?

When the buyer gives you the name, respond with:

> Thank you. Will you please let him know that I'll be calling this afternoon?

When the times comes to end the third-party relationship, be sure to tell the third-party person how appreciative you are.

> I appreciate all the effort you've put into helping me do my best for your company. I'll be sure to let your manager know what a competent assistant he has in you.

Always review the information given by the designated third party with the decision maker before presenting your recommended solution. Review the information by asking questions like this:

> According to your assistant, the company is looking for. . . .

or:

> Am I correct in my understanding of this?

Going over the information beforehand leaves you an out if you've assumed something incorrectly or if the assistant has given you any inaccurate information.

Putting yourself in your customer's shoes

Put yourself on the same level as the customer by describing yourself as consumer and telling what you go through when making decisions. When the customers realize that you also face the same kind of decisions, they'll be more open to your recommendations.

> I recently made a purchase myself. I began by gathering information and looking at various models. To be honest with you, the more I looked, the more confused I became. Finally, I decided to just go with my gut feeling and get the decision-making process over with. You know, the time we spend considering decisions is valuable, but in most cases, we usually end up going with our instincts. So I found that the quicker the decision is made, the sooner we can concentrate on other things. Is that about the way you feel, too?

If you've been working with this customer for quite some time, that little speech can knock him off the fence and get him to agree that he should just get on with it. However, if it's a major decision, this may not work. If the customer disagrees with you and just loves pondering decisions, you'll have to resort to another one of the tactics or strategies this chapter covers.

Always remember: A decision that your client attempts to put off is better than a decision that's a flat refusal!

Chapter 8
Closing the Tough Customer

. . . .

In This Chapter

▶ Using the envelope close

▶ Heading 'em off at the pass

▶ Putting other tactics to use

▶ Following up even when your prospects don't buy

. . . .

*Y*ou'll undoubtedly encounter prospective clients in your selling career who give you a tough time. In fact, you may want to think of these tough customers as professional shoppers who dedicate as much time (if not more) to mastering their craft as you do to mastering the art of closing sales. Chances are good that you'll come face to face with this type at some time or another, and when you do, it will be as if they've thrown down the gauntlet, challenging you to come up with a better reason for them to do business with you than they can come up with to take their business elsewhere. The challenge is as if they're saying, "Okay, Mr./Ms. Sales Expert, let me see your best stuff. I dare you to try to close me."

Part of the reason Joe Shopper has this attitude is that he has faced a number of salespeople in his day who have succumbed to his brashness and given him more than they would give any other client just to get his business, in which case Joe Shopper won big. Or maybe the salesperson accepted his challenge and then failed, allowing Joe Shopper to walk away to the competition with another notch in his belt.

Being able to recognize a Joe or Joanna Shopper early in your communication with him or her is crucial. You probably won't be able to spot them just by looking at them, although you can look for the following:

✔ They may carry a small notebook that they use for writing down prices while comparison shopping.

✔ They may hold an ad from one of your competitors and ask you for the same item in your store.

Without these obvious signs, though, you won't be able to tell they're professional shoppers until you begin talking with them.

Most professional shoppers won't hesitate to let you know they're looking for "the best deal," or that they're "just looking around."

After you identify the prospect as this tough type of customer, adopt a what-have-I-got-to-lose attitude, not to be confused with a devil-may-care attitude. You need to be very shrewd in determining what they really want to gain from the transaction. You also need to be very realistic and understand that you probably close only one out of every ten of these people. Customers like this are looking for a challenge as much as they are for a bargain.

So, in this chapter, I provide you with a few ways to give these customers a bit of a challenge and see if they rise to the occasion!

The Envelope, Please

For this type of situation and this type of customer, I have a close I call the *envelope close* — a challenge to your toughest customers that involves placing your best offer in an envelope, but not giving the customer the details of your offer right away.

Take a look at the following example and then examine the effectiveness. (I use a car dealership as an example of how to use the envelope close effectively.)

CHAMPION STRATEGY #1

Them: I really like the car, but I need to take a look at some other dealerships before making my decision. What's the best price you can give me on this car?

You: Okay, let me make sure I understand everything first. You're going to go to other dealers and get their investments on this car, correct? This same exact car with all the same options, same everything, right?

(Note that sales professionals use the term "investment" instead of "price" with potential clients which presents an image of gain versus loss.)

Them:	That's right! What's the best you can do for me?
You:	If I can prove to you that I will give you the best investment possible on this car, will you let us set up a date for delivery?
Them:	If you can prove you have the best price, sure!
You:	You look like a <u>man of your word</u>. I'll give you my best investment. You, however, won't believe that it's the best price until you do some shopping around, isn't that right?

Notice the underlined words "man of your word." Be sure you say this because you're going to hold the customer to his word when he returns.

Them:	That's right. I'm not saying you don't have the best price; I'm just saying I want to shop around for myself.
You:	I understand completely. I'll tell you what I can do to help you out. I'm going to write a figure on the back of my business card that is the very best price you'll find anywhere in town. Then, I'm going to put my card with your quote right here in this envelope. And so you can be assured that it won't be opened until you return, I want you to write your name across the seal. Will you do that for me?
Them:	Sure!
You:	Now, please go out and shop around. When you come back to me with a written invoice or proposal for the best investment you can find on this exact car, I'll prove to you that my investment is better. By the way, I sincerely want to save you money and do business with you for many years to come. I'll see you later.

Fast forward a couple days to when the customer comes back.

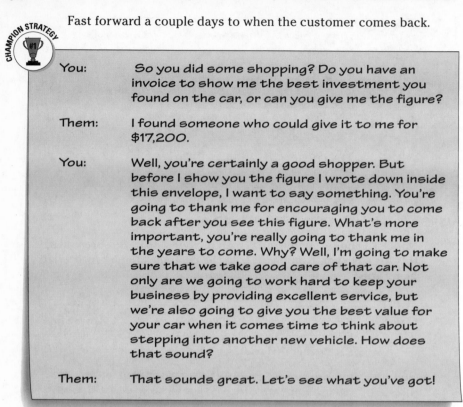

You: So you did some shopping? Do you have an invoice to show me the best investment you found on the car, or can you give me the figure?

Them: I found someone who could give it to me for $17,200.

You: Well, you're certainly a good shopper. But before I show you the figure I wrote down inside this envelope, I want to say something. You're going to thank me for encouraging you to come back after you see this figure. What's more important, you're really going to thank me in the years to come. Why? Well, I'm going to make sure that we take good care of that car. Not only are we going to work hard to keep your business by providing excellent service, but we're also going to give you the best value for your car when it comes time to think about stepping into another new vehicle. How does that sound?

Them: That sounds great. Let's see what you've got!

At this point, you open the envelope and read the figure on the card.

You: What I've written here amounts to this: Our investment is $25 less than any other amount you can find on that car. So, if you're a <u>man of your word</u> as you indicated earlier, for $17,175, you've got the car of your dreams. Congratulations!

After the customer picks his chin up off the floor, what's he going to do? If he's really the bargain shopper he professes to be, he'll admit that he's been outsmarted, grin, shake your hand, and then get down to the paperwork. And after he leaves in his brand new car, he'll tell at least three other people about his experience with you, helping you build your referral business. (If you're worried about what to do if the customer comes back with a lower figure, keep reading. I cover how to handle this in the section "Why use the envelope close?" later in the chapter.)

If you don't use the envelope close smoothly and present it as if it were a spur of the moment idea, you may look like you're begging the customers. The buyers may wonder what's wrong with your product that you must resort to such tactics to get people to buy. Then, no matter what the investment is, you've lost their confidence in you and your product.

The envelope close needs to be handled like an afterthought. Practice using the envelope close, and it won't be long before it feels quite natural when you throw it out for the customers — as an afterthought, of course.

Put your own special "lick" on the envelope close

Being creative is important throughout the sale, but is especially important during the close. You can add a special twist to the envelope close by soliciting the help of your buyer's partner (assuming the customer came in with another person). Ask the other person to be your helper. Give him a pen and a pad of paper to jot down notes as they visit other locations. Of course, make sure that the pad of paper has your name, address, and phone number printed on it. Then ask the partner to jot down a few items for comparison before they leave.

Have the helper turn the pad of paper over to the cardboard part and draw a line down the middle. On one side have him write down all the special features they're looking for in your product. On the other half, they list some of the reasons they want these features. Why put it on the cardboard? The cardboard section won't be ripped off and thrown away like it could be if it were the first page of the pad.

When you solicit the help of the buyer's partner, make sure you tell him that it's his job to be the voice of logic as they visit your competitors. Why? Every great salesperson knows that people don't buy logically — they buy emotionally. What a powerful ally this partner will be: Every time the buyer gets excited about another car, the partner will speak logically. Because you've obligated the buyer's partner and asked for his help, he will usually be quick to point out the negative features. Boom! Your buyer is slapped in the face with logic. What an emotion killer, right? Even if your store is not the first place they visit, you can use this strategy anytime your tough customers insist on doing further shopping

Here's another suggestion you may want to use with the envelope close: Before you send them out to shop around, say the following:

> You: By the way, may I ask you a question? Is our dealership the first place you visited to shop for a new car?
>
> Them: Actually, it is. You're close to our home and we saw your ad in the paper last weekend.

If the buyer says your place is the first place he's visited, but offers no explanation of what made him choose you, ask. You need his reasons for visiting you first to make this strategy work.

> You: Great! I'm going to write your reasons for visiting our dealership first on the back of my business card. If you can hand me this card when you come back in to see me, not only will I offer you the best investment in town, but I'll give you an extra bonus for having saved my card.

In offering the customer added value for keeping your card, you're assured that the buyer will remember who made him the offer and where you're located.

Make this worth his while. Be sure that the added value is enough incentive to get your customers back in to your dealership. In some areas, a car dealer gives an incentive choice of dinner for two at an uptown restaurant in the $75 to $100 range, or two movie rentals per month for one year at the local video rental store or ten $10 gift certificates for gasoline. Others send a check for $50 for every referral that ends up in a purchase.

Keep in mind the age and gender of the buyer. Movie passes may be great for a teenager, but adults may prefer a dinner for two at a neighborhood restaurant. (Make it a restaurant close to you, though, and preferably one where they have to drive past your dealership to get to it. They'll be reminded the dinner was on you — and you get more bang for your buck!)

Why use the envelope close?

The envelope close may sound like a lot of trouble to go to, but when you discover how effective it is, you'll be glad you gave this close a try. Sure, just quoting a figure and hoping for the best would be a lot easier. If this easier method is what you choose to do, you'll be in good company, because that's what most sales-people do. Ask yourself, though: What will your buyers do with that quoted figure you throw out? Exactly! They'll take that figure and use it for a comparison at every other dealership they visit. When this happens, your competitor will do just what you'd do in their place: Beat your numbers — maybe only by $25.00! The envelope close guarantees that the customer will be back because he wants to know what that figure is inside the envelope. And your competitors won't be able to beat your numbers because they have no idea what you've quoted. See the beauty of this close? The extra trouble and time is worth it.

Don't be too anxious to send your buyers shopping around. First make sure that there's no way you're going to talk the buyers into foregoing the shopping process. If it's a must for them to shop around, send them away with confidence that you've created enough curiosity to guarantee their return. The envelope close should be one of your last resorts — after you're certain they won't make a buying decision right now.

Something else you need to be aware of is the possibility that you won't have the lowest price in town. So what do you do if your buyer comes back with a lower offer? First of all, congratulate him on being such a good shopper. Let him know how rare it is that your competitors can even meet your investment, much less beat it. Then, offer added value. Now is the time to ask the customer for the card you gave him the last time he was in your office. Turn it over and look again at the reason he chose to contact your company first. If the reason is because your company is close to his home, reiterate the convenience factor of being nearby and readily available for maintenance of the vehicle.

If the buyer said he came to your dealership first because he saw your ad on television or heard it on the radio, let him know that your sales manager is very motivated to sell cars, motivated enough that if the customer were to give you the names of three friends or family members who will be purchasing a new car within the next six months, you may be able to get him an even better deal on the car, or at the very least, a referral fee or gift. Then leave your office for awhile, presumably to talk to the manager about getting a lower figure. Even if it isn't necessary for you to question your manager about additional savings, act as if you're working on the customer's behalf. Let him know you'll do everything possible to get him even better savings than what you originally quoted.

With the buyer sitting in your office waiting is no time to make sure the manager will allow you to offer a discount in the first place. Have the lowest amount that you can possibly offer on your product approved up front, before offering the lowest investment for the envelope close. Check periodically that this investment is still available if the cost of your product has a tendency to fluctuate. The last thing you want to do is offer the customers the lowest investment in town and then not be able to stand by your word.

If your buyer sends referrals to you, you may not want to use the envelope close on these new prospects. After all, you were smooth enough in the beginning to make it seem like you thought this up on the spur of the moment. If you decide to use this method of closing with the people your original buyer referred, make sure you let them know that you're willing to offer them the same opportunities to save because they were referred to you by such a good client. Make the new prospects feel as though they're being given special treatment because they were lucky enough to be referred by Mr. Buyer.

Triplicate of Choice for Money

The fact's been proven that if you give people three choices of something, they usually choose the one in the middle. Don't ask me why it works — it just does. I've tested it time and time again in my seminars by writing the numbers 1, 2, and 3 on an overhead and asking my students to choose a number. When I have those who chose the number 2 raise their hands, invariably, it's 80 percent of the audience. Even when I mix the numbers up, the one in the middle is chosen most frequently.

With this understanding, I developed what I call the *triplicate of choice for money* strategy for getting buyers to agree, before closing, on an amount of money they'd be willing to invest should they decide to go ahead and own the product or service. Having the customers agree on an amount ahead of time really helps avoid the most common money stall of saying your product or service costs too much.

(The customer may also say that she wants to think it over or that she can get the product cheaper somewhere else.)

This section provides specific, proven phraseology for you to use in each of these situations. But, knowing that most people are going to object to the cost, why not head the objection off at the pass? Why wait for it if you can avoid it altogether? Use the triplicate of choice for money closing strategy during your qualification sequence and you can eliminate the money issue and close even sooner.

This close works equally well with tangibles and intangibles. The only thing that's required is that you have three different options, including three different levels of investment for the customer.

In your qualifying sequence, ask questions about the customers' likes, dislikes, and general needs. The questioning should follow a linear pattern: Base your next questions on the answers to the previous questions, gently leading the customers toward the solution that you've determined is best for them. When you're ready to ask the money question, the one that will give you the final determination of which product they'll buy, do it this way:

You: Most people interested in acquiring a brand new washer/dryer set with all the features you've indicated you need are prepared to invest $900. A fortunate few can investment between $1,100 and $1,200. And then there are those on a limited or fixed budget who — with the high cost of everything today — can't go higher than $700. May I ask, which of these categories do you fit into most comfortably?

Most people want to be status quo, so your customers will typically choose the middle figure.

Them: Well, we were hoping it wouldn't be more than $900.

Your big surprise is that the item you're leading them to — the best solution for their needs — is the most economical one.

You:
> Then I'm excited to tell you that the model that meets your requirements requires an investment of only $700 — substantially less than you say you were prepared to invest.

What can they say? They've already said they'd invest the higher amount, so they can't come back with the objection that the product costs too much when you tell them a price that is less than what they said they could spend. You're benefiting from the psychological makeup in most people that hesitates to admit they're on a tight budget. Even if they are on a tight budget and have to admit that, you've still got them agreeing to making an investment.

To use this strategy to your best advantage, you have to know your math. You have to know the investments for your various products very well. With some practice, you can get to where you can figure out and present the formula fairly quickly in your head, but it will take practice.

CLOSE IT!

Here's the formula for developing the triplicate of choice strategy for money:

1. **State a figure that's 20 to 25 percent above the investment you think they should make.**

   The investment that you'd like them to make is the amount for the product that best satisfies their needs. Starting with a higher amount sets them up for thinking that's how much the product they've indicated they want will be.

2. **Give a range from 50 to 100 percent above the amount you think they should invest.**

   In the example earlier in this section, this was $1,100 to $1,200 amount. This is way above what you think they'll want to invest, so when you offer the next amount, the actual amount of the product they'll be happiest with, it will be somewhat of a relief.

3. **Give the actual amount as your last figure.**

   This is the amount of the product that you feel ideally suits their needs.

4. **Ask which category they fit into most comfortably.**

   Most people lean toward that middle figure, which is higher than you need to make this particular sale.

They'll commit to investing that amount of money for the product or service.

5. Respond appropriately.

If the customers choose the mid range figure, point out that the cost is substantially less than what they were prepared to invest. This is often a relief to the client because you've built their expectations for it to be a higher amount. This eliminates the money objection. They can't later say, "It costs too much," because they've already agreed to invest more than you're going to ask for in the final sale.

If the customers pick the lowest amount, remind them when it's time to close that this was exactly what they planned to spend, again eliminating the money objection.

If the customer should choose the highest amount, you may have misjudged their needs or they may be open to add-on options or services that you hadn't thought they would go for. As with any client contact, you have to be ready and willing to change your course midstream in order to give them what they expect and what will suit their needs.

At this point in the close, most people will be either ecstatic or dumbfounded. Your ecstatic customers will be happy because they can afford what they want or need. The dumbfounded response will be from those who had thought about holding out on the amount and now they can't. Either response should be followed by approval on your paperwork.

A Few More Ways to Close the Tough Guys

Some of your toughest buyers don't start out looking like they'd be tough. They're nice enough, give you a couple of common objections, but when it comes time to get their approval on the paperwork, they dig in their heels all of a sudden and bring the sales process to a screeching halt.

This situation throws many salespeople for a loop. They don't see it coming and stop dead in their tracks, not knowing what to do next. All too often, the next step they do come up with is to start discounting the product or throwing in freebies — anything to get this person to own. They may end up giving more than they get as they give away items equal or greater in value to the fee they would earn on the transaction.

Another thing these salespeople give away in situations like this is their strength. Don't risk having Freddie Freebie, as I'll call him, brag to all of his friends about all the great extras he got from you and send in ten of his best friends who also expect all the freebies. In other words, don't let the client take advantage of you. You'll be branded a pushover. Sure, you may make more sales, but at what expense?

If you're selling million-dollar aircraft and your client wants a larger TV included, that's not much of a request. However, if he wants the entire interior upgraded to leather and mahogany at no extra charge, that's another story.

Build value

Your first duty when you're faced with someone who's holding out for more than you've offered is to build the value of what they're already getting. You do this by summarizing the benefits they've already agreed to and talking about the emotional and financial value of those benefits.

You: I can appreciate your hesitation. However, let me reiterate the benefits you're gaining by joining our fitness center today. With the plan you've indicated works best for you, you're getting 18 months of additional membership for an up front investment of only two years' service. You're receiving three private sessions with a personal trainer, which is something you indicated would be especially beneficial in getting you started, isn't that right? Our trainers are certified, and on their own time could demand up to $75 per hour for these services.

The cleanliness of a health facility is very important to our reputation. Our fitness centers are required to surpass the standards deemed necessary by the Health Department. In fact, we have an 80-point checklist that our service people must review on the cleanliness of the sink areas alone. That checklist is completed and filed every 48 hours.

All of our equipment is state of the art, and we evaluate the usage of each piece of equipment on a monthly basis. If something is in high demand, we'll replace another machine that's not used as often with a duplicate of the more popular one, so you should rarely, if ever, have to wait to use a piece of equipment. That was one of your concerns, wasn't it?

With your initial membership, we'll include three 10-day passes for friends or relatives of yours to join you at the club so you'll have workout buddies right away. I'm sure whoever you choose to use these passes will be very appreciative. We offer over 40 classes each week, again with certified instructors, in the areas of aerobic training and self-defense so you should be able to fit those you are interested in into your busy schedule, don't you think? Now, what aspects of a club were you expecting that we may be missing? Where we could better serve your particular needs?

When you do a summary like that, it will seem pretty silly for the client to hold out for a free water bottle or T-shirt. If they do, however, insist on something extra, go with whatever your manager allows.

Empower your buyers

One of the biggest complaints buyers have is that they feel out of control in the buying process, which makes the process an unpleasant experience for them. The more expensive the product or service, the more important it is to empower your buyers. After you've identified the decision maker, give that person the power to make the decision to own your product or service. Be the expert advisor, the decision counselor — not the controller. If the customers want to shop around, let them know that you think that's the best idea yet. Encourage them to trust their own decisions.

Tough buyers enjoy participating in the negotiations. Getting the best price isn't really good enough. They may not want to be given anything; rather, they want to earn the best investment. Making the buyers players in the negotiations process empowers them: They believe that it was because of their efforts — and that they were smart enough and clever enough — that they got such a great deal. They'll feel great if they think they got the best of you. Buyers feel like the salesperson is really out to take their money, so let them feel like they have the upper hand. To really make the customers feel good, ask for double the number of referrals and say it's because you need them to make up for the beating you took at their hands. Do this and watch them puff up! The best part is that they *will* send you double the referrals because they feel wonderful about your product and their abilities as a negotiator.

Follow Up Even If the Buyers Don't Buy

Expect success when closing, but should success elude you for a short while, practice great follow-up. If you're not following up now on resistant buyers, you should be. Some salespeople think resistant means nonexistent. A hesitant buyer can mean a number of things: perhaps you moved a little too fast, failed to give enough information, gave too much information, didn't recognize the customer's hot buttons (benefits they want to own), or forgot to qualify. Whatever the reason for resistance to the close, there's usually a solution to the problem — if you're a persistent salesperson.

What are some of the ways you can follow up with customers who resist your attempts? Make a phone call. Don't assume they've purchased from your competitor. Resistant buyers are just as difficult for your competition to handle as they are for you. So instead of feeling defeated when you make your follow-up call, assume that the customer hasn't been able to make a decision yet and that you're going to be the one to change his mind.

If your buyer is a corporate account, you may want to try an e-mail message or fax. Add a little urgency to your message. If your product or service is a limited offering, you may want to reinforce this and encourage the buyer to get in touch with you immediately. (Check out Chapter 12 for more on following up.)

Follow-up after an attempted close is probably one of the most difficult things to do for the less experienced salesperson. If you think of yourself as a failure because the buyers didn't come back after such a creative close, you need to look at things with a different perspective. Of course you want to close and you want to be a winner, but every selling opportunity won't end in a sale. But not every selling situation ends with the first no, either. Almost every no or maybe can be changed to a yes with the right motivation and strategies.

So develop strong follow-up skills and practice them on a consistent basis. The only way to become a good closer is to close.

Chapter 9

Remote Closing

- -

In This Chapter

▶ Phoning your way to success

▶ Faxing doesn't have to be taxing

▶ Remote closing with network marketing

▶ Living in e-mail heaven

▶ Closing online

- -

*R*emote closing benefits you whether you're involved in network marketing, selling from your home office, or closing a transaction with a client who's across the country or even the ocean.

In the past, most companies divided territories by geographical area. Today, many salespeople specialize in particular products or services and concentrate on clients who have needs that match the product. So, companies are more likely to claim as your territory any client who has a need for your specialty. That means your client base may quite literally be anywhere in the world. If that's the case with you, you'll do very little face-to-face selling and a whole lot of remote closing.

What do you do when you're not closing face-to-face? Well, when you close from a distance, you call upon your skills as a closer and rely on the wonders of technology like phones, fax machines, the Internet, e-mail, and express or overnight delivery services.

Closing by Phone

Okay, I'm going to start out with an example to help show you the best way to close by phone. Say you've presented to International, Inc. in Los Angeles, and you're back in the home office in Boise. Your presentation was precisely detailed. You established great rapport with the three committee members and followed up with thank-you notes to each individual before you left L.A. They told you they had to make a decision by today. What are your chances of getting the agreement? Very good if you answer yes to the following questions:

✔ Did you call either yesterday or the day before to check and see if the clients had any remaining questions about the ability of your product to satisfy their needs?

✔ Did you arrange a specific time for their call today? Hopefully yes because if you didn't, you're risking the results of this huge contract being shuffled off to the realm of voice mail.

✔ Have you reread your entire file on this account so all the details are fresh in your mind?

✔ Do you have your brief summary review (your list of everything they agreed that they like about your product) filled with emotional involvement phrases — ones that help them know what they'll feel *after* they take ownership of the product — on hand for the call?

✔ Does your receptionist or secretary know to hold all other calls at the appointed time and to preannounce the clients' call to you?

✔ Do you have a solid closing question — one that asks for a firm commitment today — prepared and rehearsed?

Every yes you answer here brings you closer to getting the big yes from your clients. Even if the potential clients dismissed you in L.A. with a "we'll get back with you," that doesn't mean you sit and stay like a good little puppy until they call you. You're a professional. Be proactive. Calling a day or two before the decision to see if anything new has come up doesn't make you a pest. Making this call is a courtesy — a professional courtesy — and a way to protect your interest in the clients. You can bet the competition is trying to lobby for their product, so why shouldn't you?

If your clients say they'll get back to you, immediately use your closing abilities to arrange a specific time to visit with them by telephone. (Of course, the time must best suit their needs. If they're in Singapore, that could mean you need to be ready for the call at a pretty odd hour in Boise.) Establishing a specific time keeps you from wasting a day staying off the phone in case they call.

CHAMPION STRATEGY #1

| You: | I know you plan on making a decision by next Thursday. Can you tell me if you have a morning or afternoon deadline? |
| Them: | We need to submit the accepted proposal to the finance department before noon. |

> **You:** That's great. Then I can expect a call from you before noon on Thursday?
>
> **Them:** I guess so.
>
> **You:** I know how important this investment is to International, Inc., and how valuable your time is. To ensure that I'm available to you, and in case there are any details we need to discuss further, shall we arrange a telephone call at 11:00 on Thursday, or would 11:15 be better?

What have you got to lose by trying this? Not much. If the clients can promise to call at a certain time, you'll be at your best when they call because you're expecting it and you've prepared. If the clients can't give you a certain time, you've at least shown your determination to serve by trying to make these arrangements.

Never risk having a closing call go to voice mail. Hearing a recorded message makes it easy for a client to tell you no. If the clients have to give you their answers in person — in this case, meaning voice-to-voice — they have to at least allow you the courtesy of asking a few questions regarding the decision, which may open that window of opportunity right back up.

If you're the one making the call to hear their decision, you still have to be just as prepared as if they were calling you. (And, of course, you still have to arrange and confirm the time for the call.)

Never, never, *never* begin a closing telephone conversation with, "I'm calling for your decision." Mistakes like this are selling suicide.

Always try to have a new or interesting tidbit of information at the ready when you make the closing call. A tidbit is especially powerful when it relates to something the clients mentioned in a previous conversation.

> **You:** Hi, this is (your name here). How are you doing today?
>
> **Them:** Okay. How about you?

(continued)

(continued)

> You: Just great. In fact, I'm excited about something new I have to share with you regarding our X-Pro voice mail system. I know you had some concerns about your staff getting their messages on those days when they're off site. I spoke with our technical services department and they have come up with a way to modify that feature on the system to reduce it from a three-step process to only two steps for your people to retrieve their messages from any location. Isn't that great?

What have you done? You've already gone the extra mile for this client even before they made a decision to own your product or service. The hinges on that door he or she thought about closing are beginning to creak, thanks to your preparedness and professionalism.

Holding the customer's attention

Because the ears and only one small part of the brain are focused on listening, you must plan for your telephone conversation to include all the senses used in a face-to-face conversation. By incorporating as many senses as possible into your conversation, you're better able to hold the customer's attention.

✔ Visually engage your clients by faxing material to them before you call. Be sure they receive it in plenty of time to review it thoroughly before the call.

By faxing a list of benefits the buyers will enjoy after they own your product or service, you visually involve the prospect by referring to the faxed benefit list during the conversation.

✔ Another visual way to engage your customer is to use face-to-face teleconferencing. Many businesses and some hotels offer this service to meet the needs of their clients — people like you. This service is even available through the Internet, but you have to have a small camera on each end for the visual transmission.

✔ To get your customers thinking a little, ask if they can name any other benefits in addition to the ones on the benefits list.

> ✔ To engage the sense of touch, ask your customers to use a calculator to figure the savings they'll enjoy with your product.

Again, the goal here is to hold the customers' attention. By asking them questions, giving them something to look at, and having them do calculations, you make them an active participant — and they give you their full attention.

One of the most effective remote closing strategies is to tie in a third party through a conference call. The third party can be a technical specialist who can address technical concerns or a satisfied customer who can add valuable information.

Drawing the customer a pretty picture

When closing by telephone, use language that creates a picture to keep the customer's mind engaged. For example, use fun and interesting adjectives like:

> ✔ Stylish

As you can see in the catalog, our new CS5000 printer has a sleek, stylish design that takes up less of your valuable desktop space.

> ✔ Airy

Understanding that size is an important consideration for retirees, our condominium designers have added ceiling height, skylights, and plenty of windows to make even the smaller model homes have an airy, open feeling.

> ✔ Time-saving

With the latest version of this software, we've added many time-saving features. Never again will your staff have to reformat the fields of your mailing lists to match the word processing feature. The software will automatically read over 100 standard formats.

✔ Spacious

CHAMPION STRATEGY #1

> All of our hotel suites have spacious living areas, which include office setups with fax modems or Internet lines available upon request.

✔ Cost-effective

CHAMPION STRATEGY #1

> Can you see how the larger print run of these brochures will be more cost-effective, especially if you see yourself using these pieces for the entire year?

✔ Efficient

CHAMPION STRATEGY #1

> The upgrade of your mailing equipment will streamline the process, thus making your staff more efficient in handling your larger marketing mailers.

✔ Morale-boosting

CHAMPION STRATEGY #1

> An increase of this sort in the amount of coverage you place on each member of your staff will have a tremendous morale-boosting effect. And most of our clients find a tremendous increase in productivity after implementing such a change.

✔ Fabulous

CHAMPION STRATEGY #1

> The implementation of this new training program has brought about fabulous increases in bottom-line revenues for the last six clients I've worked with.

✔ Excellent

> Our customer service department has consistently received an excellent rating from our existing clients in the Customer Satisfaction Surveys that we conduct every year.

✔ Powerful

> The new chip in our Compu-Plus computers makes them the most powerful units available today. And added power means it will run your software faster and more efficiently, which is something your entire staff would appreciate, isn't it?

You can also use analogies and examples from satisfied customers. If your client is a sports fan this should be easy. If they hate all sports, but have kids, use the kid angle. No kids? How about pets? Interest in movies? Everyone has an interest that can be used in an analogy or related example if you just keep searching for it.

✔ You can compare the business to the local winning team no matter the sport. If the client is a fan of a particular team, use that team in your analogy as to how they plan, strategize, and practice to become winners.

✔ If your product involves future positive results and your clients have kids, talk about how fast those kids grow and how one small change made today can have a powerful impact on their futures.

✔ Watch for and make notes of satisfied clients and be ready to tell their success stories to each new client.

Every top professional in the field of selling is a collector of stories, facts, and figures from actual clients. This collection is often their most valuable tool in getting new clients on board.

Getting your message across

When you're closing over the phone, you have to work a little harder to get your message across. Speaking to someone over the phone diminishes your message — and your voice. You have to project your voice, enthusiasm, and upbeat personality — sort of like a theater actor projects from the stage. By projecting, I mean that the loudness, tone, and inflection of your voice needs to be amplified a bit in order for your voice to carry at the optimum level. Here are a couple tips:

🖋 **Don't — by any means — shout your message.**

Shouting is reserved for rooftops. Speaking too loudly into the telephone is irritating to listeners, and you can damage both your image in their eyes and the drums in their ears.

🖋 **Do, however, speak up and speak clearly.**

When leaving a voice mail, speak clearly and at a slow pace, so that the person listening to the message will not have to replay your message in order to return your call. Luckily, the technology is in place for the recipient to replay messages easily, but you don't want to do anything to cause frustration, especially when you're near to closing time.

Putting on your happy face

Telephone conversations can bore your customer if you don't vary the tone of your voice. To maintain the prospect's interest in the conversation, be extra enthusiastic and above all, *smile*. The person on the other end won't be able to see your smile, but believe me, the customer can tell whether you're smiling or frowning over the phone lines. People can tell when you're happy to be talking with them and that makes them feel good — and that's what you want when you're closing. Even if you're having a tough day, it's not fair to that person on the other end of the line if you let it affect your communication with them. Pros have mastered how to put any other challenges aside when talking with clients.

When I was a manager, I put little mirrors by every telephone in the sales area. My people couldn't talk on the phone without noticing whether or not they were smiling. Of course, we had them take down the mirrors if clients came through on tours, but having the mirrors was a great reminder. When our training firm built a telemarketing division, we put large 8-inch square mirrors in every cubicle directly in front of the telemarketer. Many of those telemarketers have since moved on but still use the mirror strategy in their businesses today.

I know of a few companies who have used the smiley face stickers or just taped the word "smile" to the base of the telephones their sales and customer service people use. For those using headsets or working at computers with client information, put it right on the top of their computer screens!

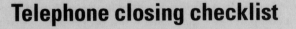

Telephone closing checklist

✔ Amplify your voice.

✔ Speak clearly.

✔ Don't rush (especially when leaving voice mail messages).

✔ Stand.

✔ Smile.

✔ Dress professionally.

✔ Vary your tone and inflection.

✔ Use picture-drawing words.

✔ Conference in a third party.

Many professional salespeople who market their products or services over the telephone find it helpful to stand when talking to clients. Standing gives them more energy, which is reflected in their voices. Standing straight also eliminates the tendency to slouch, which does nothing good for your voice transmission.

Another good point is that even if you're working from home and contacting clients all around the world, dress the part. Chances are, if you spend the day in your jammies, you're going to have a more relaxed mindset. That's good on creative days; it's bad when talking with clients. I know of many salespeople who work from home, yet everyday they get up, shower, and dress as if they're working in a professional office, then walk the few feet to their desks and conduct business in a professional manner. You may not need to do this to acquire and maintain a professional attitude, but if it helps, why not do it? You may laugh at this, but I've even recommended to some people that they go so far as to go out to the driveway, back the car out and pull back in as if they've just arrived for work. For those who are somewhat new to working from home, this can be a poweful strategy to get your day started on the right foot.

One good thing about closing by phone is that great strides have been made in the quality of telephone communication in recent years, and even though you may prefer face-to-face communication, many professional salespeople earn high commissions through remote closing. Doing business over the phone may have drawbacks, but with the proper attitude and a few powerful strategies, you can turn them into advantages.

For Network Marketers

The closing strategies throughout this book work beautifully in network marketing. *Network marketing* — when you're involved with a company as a distributor of their products or service — has also been called *multi-level marketing*. Your involvement entitles you to offer your same opportunity to others and you can earn an income from their sales as well as from your own.

The bottom line is that you can build an organization of which you are the leader without having to come up with your own product or even your own marketing strategy. The product and marketing materials are already in place for you, and the companies are simply seeking representatives to bring their products to market. You may have heard of some of the larger network marketing companies such as Amway, Nu Skin, and Discovery Toys. Their network marketers build distributorships, nationally and internationally. Some of the top people in their companies have huge organizations around the world — with very few distributors in their local areas. Some have literally thousands of people in their organizations whom they have never met face-to-face.

By using remote closing techniques, you can help potential recruits understand — emotionally and otherwise — how they'll benefit from your network marketing opportunity. The use of conference calling (or three-way calling) can be especially effective.

For example, suppose you're fairly new to the business and want to persuade your cousin in Chicago to join your network marketing organization. You live in Dallas. There are no family reunions or holidays on the horizon, so you have to do this over the telephone. You've already called and built his interest with your enthusiasm and excitement. However, your skeptical cousin wants to hear from someone who's been in the business for awhile and see how she's doing. You make arrangements with a successful person in your network to get on a three-way call with you. You make the introductions and let the successful network marketer answer your cousin's questions. After she addresses all of his concerns, you take control of the conversation and close.

If you're really new at the selling game, you can arrange for the successful network marketer to close for you and you simply handle the paperwork and follow-up. Listen and learn from the experienced network marketer. The next time you have an opportunity to recruit someone to your organization, use this successful closer's strategies.

Here's a good closing question for my network marketing friends:

> **Who are the first three people you're going to present the product and opportunity to?**

When the potential recruit starts thinking about his list of prospects rather than his previous concerns, he's closed.

Fax Closing Strategies

If you've closed over the telephone — or you're just about to close — but your client needs to review some paperwork, chances are you'll be using a fax machine for your remote close. You may need to send them the final agreement so they have a hard copy for signatures. Your clients may want to clarify some of the legal aspects of the agreement if it's a large sale and, of course, this needs to be in writing.

Because you want your faxed document to get to the right person, always send the fax with a cover sheet. The *cover sheet* is a top sheet that includes the name of the person that the fax is for, the number of pages that the fax includes, and a sentence that identifies the information in the fax — something like "requested information," "requested quotation," or "new information about how to. . . ."

One client received three pages of information but made the decision to go with another firm. The fourth page of the transmission was missing and that's where the salesperson put the discount schedule for that client. Oops — big oops! Be sure to *always* use a cover sheet.

I strongly recommend that you follow up every fax with a quick phone call to ensure that the recipient really did receive the information, that it transmitted clearly, and that they have all the pages. Your follow-up call shows your concern for details and also gives you an opportunity to move right into the close. For example:

> **And by the way, while I've got you on the telephone, I'd be happy to review this with you now, while we both have the facts and figures right in front of us.**

I also recommend that you include a single summary page with any fax of more than three pages. The summary page should be in large print and list explicitly what the recipient has and what he or she needs to do with it.

Using E-Mail

E-mail is part of the most recent revolution in how people communicate. E-mail is simply a software program that allows you, with a modem, to send written messages — and even attached photos or large written documents — to someone else's computer. E-mail is fast and easy, and more and more salespeople are using it in their daily work because it's fast, it's easy, and used effectively, it can help you close the sale.

If you're closing using e-mail, prepare your document as you would draft a formal letter or proposal. Use bullet points, summaries, and a bit of white space — that is, blanks between salient points to make your e-mail as eye appealing as possible.

✔ You can use all caps for section headlines and extra spacing between sections or important points for appearance's sake or for emphasis.

✔ Be certain you print out a copy of the document for yourself and have it proofread — preferably by someone else with a really good eye — before you send it. As with anything you write, you may be so close to the material, knowing what you want it to say, that you believe you've covered everything, but have minor typographical errors in the writing. Most importantly, have someone else double-check any figures you put into a document. Showing poor math to clients will put a huge dent in your credibility with them.

Because of the speed of e-mail, I find that people don't check their work as well as they should. They tend to get excited that they can answer clients' needs so fast that they do it without taking professional precautions. For example, I've received several proposals with either no phone numbers or incorrect phone numbers, so we couldn't call with our questions. I had to send an e-mail back and then wait, which is not the most efficient way to handle business.

If much of your communication with potential clients is via e-mail, be especially careful about the wording you use. In person, the client picks up on your tone, inflection, and body language as part of your message. E-mail depersonalizes communication to a great extent, so if you decide to include verbiage that reflects your personality, make certain it's appropriate. If in doubt, run it by your manager or supervisor.

One of my students, Craig Valine, has rave reviews for using e-mail in closing sales. He finds that many of his business owner prospects are hard to reach during the business day, so he gets their e-mail addresses and follows up that way. He feels that clients really think through their questions and concerns when they have to write them down. He receives concise information from the clients with little or no emotion attached — sort of a "just the facts, ma'am" reply listing the features they're looking for. Craig then has the advantage of being able to think and carefully draft his replies, building in the emotional benefits. With e-mail, he accomplishes two things:

- ✔ A comprehensive transfer of information.

- ✔ Time-saving efficiency over trying to connect by phone or hoping the business owner receives and reads their faxes in a timely manner.

Craig also finds that the fears face-to-face clients have about facing a salesperson and investing valuable time in decision-making meetings are lessened with e-mail clients. Additionally, the wait between the time of transmission and reply also distances clients from some of the instinctive fears that arise in selling situations. (I talk a lot about those fears in Chapter 6.)

Internet Closing

If you're not yet familiar with the features and power of using the Internet, I strongly recommend you pick up a copy of *The Internet For Dummies,* 5th Edition, by John R. Levine, Carol Baroudi, and Margaret Levine Young (IDG Books Worldwide, Inc.). After you get online and see how others are using this tool, you'll undoubtedly be inspired to use it for yourself.

The possibilities are practically endless when it comes to closing on the Internet. Seeing the innovative ideas people are coming up with on their Web sites is always interesting and goes to show that the sky is the limit. As with any marketing tool, the Internet should not be left to stand alone; it needs support. Here are some simple rules to follow when developing your site:

- ✔ You need to advertise that you have a Web site. You can use traditional advertising methods such as radio, television, or print media, or simply print your Web address on all of your materials, including business cards, letterhead, e-mail, fax cover sheets, and so on. What you choose will depend upon your particular advertising budget.

✔ Your home page needs to be attractive and draw people through the information that's there.

✔ The site should entice the viewer into wanting your product or service and include a call to action for them to place an order.

✔ Users need to be able to contact you easily via e-mail, toll free phone numbers, and fax numbers to get prompt answers to any questions they may have before placing an order.

✔ Order forms should be easy to fill out.

✔ Transactions must be secure. This means that if customers are sending you a credit card number or other financial data over the Internet, you've taken steps to prevent others from gaining access to it.

✔ You must have a system in place to acknowledge orders. Some companies manually send a brief reply to anyone placing an order. Others have a capability built-in to their sites that sends acknowledgments as soon as the transmission is complete.

Many people today are finding shopping on the Internet to be ideal. They can find what they want, "window shop" for new ideas, place orders, and never leave their desk or have to talk with a salesperson. The Internet is the next generation after catalog shopping — with one of the biggest advantages being that there's nothing to recycle.

If you're using your site as an online catalog, you can do one better than print by showing your products in a three-dimensional mode. If your product includes audio or video, you can demo it through the computer.

One of my students, John Songdahl, had his salespeople use the company Web site as an instant brochure for potential customers who asked to be sent something, which led to having a demo of the company's product available online for a 30-day test drive.

Providing a demo is a strategy called the puppy dog close in sales training. Your clients actually use the product or service before they agree to own it. The idea behind the strategy is that after they use the product and are used to it, they'll wonder how they ever did without it — and then agree to the purchase. How do you find new homes for cute little puppies? You send them home with the children. In this case, after a family has the demo for a few days, they become emotionally involved and just can't return it.

When the time comes to close the sale, John sends out a preclose e-mail to open the door. In his e-mail he says:

Mr. Practitioner,

Thank you for taking the opportunity to try our new "Checkpoint" research service. We are extremely excited to offer the latest breaking (tax, accounting, HR) news to your desktop the moment it happens.

As you know, this is relatively new technology and an evolutionary product for us. We're always looking to the people we serve for ways to make our research products meet their individual and changing needs. I will contact you in a few days and would be interested in hearing your feedback and comments on the following question:

If you had the opportunity to tailor this product specifically to your business, what would you change or add to the service?

I look forward to speaking with you.

The purpose of this correspondence is to get the customer to identify his hot button or major area of concern. Most of the time, the hot button — that is, a benefit your customer has already indicated he wants to own — is something the service already does, but the customer hasn't discovered that yet, which gives the representative the opportunity to turn the customer's reply into a close by demonstrating that particular feature.

If it's appropriate for your particular product, think about putting your entire presentation online. Of course, with an in-person presentation you're able to customize, but having your fine-tuned presentation available for potential new clients to view can lead to some pretty easy closes when you make direct contact with them.

The best way to determine if your product is appropriate for online sales is to see how many of your competitors are using the Internet as a sales tool and try to determine how well they're doing with it. This can be as easy as calling up or e-mailing one of their salespeople, telling him or her that you're doing research on the Internet (no lie, because you are), and ask how sales are for them. If no one else with your particular product is online, it may not be the best avenue for your particular product or service.

Another consideration would be to consult with a company that creates Web pages and get some preliminary suggestions from them as to how they see you succeeding on the Internet with your product or service. Of course, if you decide to go ahead with them, you'll pay a fee for building your site and managing it, but if they're really experts, they'll know ways to make it work for you.

Part III
Continuing to Build Your Business

The 5th Wave   By Rich Tennant

"I think you're still giving away too much for the close, Ms. Lamont."

In this part...

In this part, you find out how to maximize your business with every client contact, create more business through existing clients, build customer loyalty through competent service, and — if necessary — discover how to bow out gracefully if your product isn't right for your clients (but get referrals anyway!).

Chapter 10

Keeping the Sale Closed

. . . .

In This Chapter

▶ Figuring out if yes really means yes

▶ Conquering buyer's remorse

▶ Making sure your sale stays closed

. . . .

*F*iguring out how to close the sale isn't enough — now you have to keep the sale closed. Keeping the sale closed involves giving the new client ownership of the product or service in every possible way, shape, and form that you can come up with, as quickly as possible.

 ✔ If you don't carry your inventory with you, you have to arrange for delivery or installation of the product. The sooner you do this, the better.

 ✔ If you do have the product on hand, as you're handing it over to the client, talk with them about how they'll enjoy it — and who they'll be showing it off to — but do it in terms of the product being theirs not yours.

 For example, if your client has just invested in new patio furniture, as you're helping them load it in their truck, say, "Your patio will look great with this new furniture. How soon will you be entertaining your friends out there?" This will have the new owners visualizing their friends enjoying themselves and the new furniture will be the focal point of that picture.

Depending on the customers, the type of product or service, and the salesperson, to put and keep a transaction together can require several negotiations and closes. Good salespeople know that there's no relaxing and that the sale cannot be put to bed until a reasonable period of time has elapsed after the sale has been consummated. The reasonable time frame varies for different people and different products or services.

 ✔ For real estate, the time frame may be as long as six months before ownership of the home actually changes hands and the new owners are moved in. A lot can happen in that time period to change the course of the sale.

✔ For most major purchases, there's at least a 72-hour period in which consumers can change their minds — and many do.

✔ Even in the everyday retail environment, refunds and exchanges may be made within 30 days.

The more ownership feelings you create during the initial presentation and close, the better. After your client leaves you, they're going to see friends and relatives and talk with them about their purchase, especially if it's a major one. The reactions of those friends to the purchase can cause the client to have second thoughts about ownership. That's why you have to build excitement for the purchase and help the client envision themselves already owning it before they leave you.

"It's Not What They Say..."

Top closers know that a simple yes isn't always enough to get prospects to assume ownership. Going back to the old saying, "It's not what you say, but how you say it that counts," you need to be able to read what the customers mean by how they say that yes. Say the product is a water system — softener and reverse osmosis drinking filter. If you hear, "Yes, let's go ahead," that's one thing. If it's, "Yes, let's get that new water softener installed. I can't wait to feel that soft water in the shower," that's a whole different story. If you hear the former type of yes, you need to add emotional appeal to your chitchat as you fill out the paperwork to build their emotional attachment to the product. If you hear the latter type of yes, you need only to smile encouragingly and maybe give a few tie downs (see Chapter 5) to their statements to build ownership.

Let me show you the difference and how to handle each type of yes. When the customer needs some encouragement, follow this example:

CHAMPION STRATEGY

Them:	Yes, let's go ahead.
You:	That's great. Let's get the paperwork out of the way so I can get that new unit scheduled for installation. Won't it be great to get a drink of purified water right from your sink rather than lugging those big jugs around?

> Them: Yes. It'll be easier on my wife, too, because she couldn't lift them and had to wait for me to get home to change the jugs.
>
> You: It sounds like you'll both be pretty happy with this new unit, won't you?

And so on. The idea here is to get the customer to mention the reasons he is going ahead with the purchase.

For those clients who are already pretty excited, you can take the shorter conversational road:

> Them: Yes, let's get that new water softener installed. I can't wait to feel that soft water in the shower.
>
> You: Won't that be great?
>
> Them: Yeah, and having drinking water right at the sink is a bonus.
>
> You: I can see you're happy with this decision. With your approval right here, I'll get out of your way and get the installation scheduled.

If your clients are already this committed, the sooner you move on to arranging delivery and installation, the better. Get the paperwork and financial aspects handled, and then get out of there — allow the new owners to relish the wise decision they've just made.

Overcoming Buyer's Remorse

Buyer's remorse — the second thoughts, hesitation, or regret that buyers sometimes feel — is a common feeling buyers experience, especially after making a purchase that requires a large investment. When you understand the cause of buyer's remorse and anticipate it, you can prepare yourself to counter those feelings, to reassure your new clients that they've made a wise decision, and to let them know that buyer's remorse is a normal feeling.

Making the intangible tangible

During the first few minutes/hours/days after making a decision, many new clients start second-guessing themselves. What's really happening is that their focus is turning to the loss of their security (money) instead of the benefits of ownership, which is why it's called buyer's *remorse*. It's up to you to head off buyer's remorse off by preparing the client for it in advance. This preparation can be tricky when your product or service is an intangible or is not immediately available, but it can be done.

Intangibles are products or services like insurance or ad space, marketing ideas, education, or services such as janitorial services. Intangible products are more difficult to build value into because positive results must be imagined or envisioned by the customer; they cannot be experienced through the senses. What you have to do with intangible products and services is enable the buyers to experience them by helping them picture the benefits.

✔ "Just think how well you'll sleep tonight, knowing that you've secured your children's future education with this policy."

✔ "Can't you just see the beauty of this ad and how its placement will bring your business just the recognition you want?"

✔ "Imagine yourself coming home from a tough day at work and walking into a house that's clean with the beds made and the garbage all taken out. You can just kick off your shoes and relax."

Notice that not one of these statements mentions money. The focus is changed from what the customers are giving to what they're getting. You have to change your focus, too, from it's-a-closed-sale-let-your-guard-down attitude to it-may-not-be-closed-steel-edged-let's-keep-it-closed attitude. You've got to focus and then get the customers focused on what they're *gaining* by investing their money instead of what they're *giving* to get ownership. There's power in ownership, so help the customer experience that power.

The following are just a few of the things that can contribute to buyer's remorse:

- ✔ **A feeling of loss.** In our society, money is a form of security, and for many of us, it's the highest form of security. When you ask clients to make buying decisions, you're asking them to give up some of their security. Remember this point whenever you prepare to close a sale. Have you built enough emotional security into the new whatzit you're asking them to own? Have you made the product more valuable to them than the money/security they're being asked to give up?

- ✔ **Well-meaning yet mistaken advice.** One of the first things your customer is going to do after he buys a product is show it off. The inherent risk of showing off things is hearing comments — some good and some maybe not so good. Hearing one negative comment or some misguided advice can initiate a round of second-guessing, causing your consumer to return the purchase.

- ✔ **Logic comes into play.** What happens here is that the customer begins to analyze the details instead of enjoying the feeling. Few people buy products or services logically; they buy emotionally, and then defend their decisions with logic. In the case of someone suffering from buyer's remorse, he's having trouble finding a great logic to defend his emotional purchase. In other words, the customer doesn't have a strong enough emotional attachment to the product.

Helping customers avoid buyer's remorse

Some salespeople choose to bring up the after-the-sale objection right away in order to best prepare the buyer for what may occur after they get home. Dealing with buyer's remorse may involve some risk, but if you've received any indication that your customers have reservations, you must learn and use the following phraseology (which is also a must when dealing with a large sale):

You:	I can tell that you feel good about your decision to own this beautiful television. You're excited and somewhat relieved to have finally made the decision to receive hours of enjoyment from it, aren't you?

(continued)

(continued)

Them:	Well, I am looking forward to getting it home and watching the football game on a big screen!
You:	That's great! (Pause) From time to time, I have had people just like you who were so positive about the decision they made until they shared it with a friend or relative. The well-meaning friends or relatives, not understanding all the facts and maybe even being a little envious, discouraged them from their decision for one reason or another. Please don't let this happen to you. In fact, if you think you may change your mind, please, tell me now.

By following this sample dialogue, you give the customer a way out, but it's at a time when he is still emotionally affected by ownership. And what will most likely occur is that he'll deny having any doubts right now and review in his mind all the reasons he's going ahead with the purchase (which creates more attachment to the product). You've also prepared the customer for buyer's remorse and he'll likely remember what you said if he should hear any discouragement from friends or relatives.

Using this phraseology has been proven in hundreds of cases to open up customers and get them to talk about doubts they may have, which enables you to immediately face the task of keeping the sale closed while you're still with them. If you don't find out about these doubts until after you consider the sale closed, say hours or days later, it's much harder for you to keep that sale closed. The prospective client will have had too much time to rationalize why he shouldn't own your product or service and you'll be back at square one: having to rebuild rapport, requalify, review product benefits, readdress concerns and redo the close. In other words, you'll have to bring them to the point of feeling ownership all over again.

Changing the customer's tune

Knowing how strong a part buyer's remorse plays in selling situations, you need to discover ways to keep your buyers excited about the decisions they make. If the customers come back to you two days after a large computer purchase demanding their money back, don't get hysterical. (Remaining calm is the first rule of thumb.) The more concerned you are about losing the commission on a sale, the more obstinate your customers will be in their demands to get a full money-back refund. So stay calm and do what's necessary to keep the sale closed. Here's an idea of what to say:

Them:	This computer just isn't working out for us. We'd like our money back.
You:	It isn't working out? You were so excited two days ago. Would you mind telling me what has happened since then that would cause you to change your mind?
Them:	Well, we just can't get it to run the programs from our old machine, and they're the ones we really need. So if it won't run them, we don't want it.
You:	I see. The challenge is in getting your existing information onto the new machine, right?
Them:	Yes, that's it. If we'd known it would be this difficult, we wouldn't have considered getting a newer computer. We thought a newer machine would allow us to do more, not restrict what we're already doing.
You:	If I recall correctly, you have an older operating system on your other machine, don't you?
Them:	I guess it would have to.
You:	The challenge you're having may not be with the equipment as much as the operating system. Many times when a new operating system is released, software companies will upgrade their programs to work better with that operating system. When was the last time you upgraded any of your software?
Them:	Not for a long time.
You:	Do you enjoy the programs you're now using enough to upgrade them?

(continued)

(continued)

> **Them:** Yeah, they work well for us and we're used to them.
>
> **You:** That's great, and upgrades will have more features on them that you'll undoubtedly find useful without having to learn whole new programs. However, many of the more recent versions of software will require the newer operating system to run.
>
> **Them:** So, we're back to needing the new computer in order to use the better versions.

You've come full circle with your client. They're not necessarily emotionally attached once again to the new computer. However, they're probably beginning to rationalize keeping the computer instead of asking for that refund. How did you change their tune? You dialed another station. You changed their focus from what the computer wouldn't do to what it will do for them in the future.

Always remember that high-tech equipment has tremendous future value. Ownership automatically takes people into the future compared to where they were just prior to ownership.

Ways to Keep the Sale Sold

Specific strategies, when applied properly, can greatly assist you in solidifying the sale. The following sections introduce these strategies. Begin applying them today and watch your cancellations dwindle.

Offering benefits that build commitment

As an example to illustrate this point, say you're an entrepreneur with a cleaning service. Your goal is to get the client to commit to a 12-month agreement. Not having concrete proof that you do the phenomenal job you've been selling, the customer may hesitate to make such a long commitment. To overcome this hesitancy, consider including a 30-day trial period in your agreements. If after 30 days your customer isn't totally satisfied with your cleaning services, the agreement may be canceled with no additional fees. Make sure the client recognizes the fact that only companies that are very confident of their services can make this offer. (If you have a history of 30-day cancellations, you simply couldn't afford it.) This tactic will make your client more comfortable with committing to the full 12-month agreement as she has a way out if she's not satisfied; it will help keep the sale closed.

Another benefit that builds commitment is offering a loaner, if applicable. For example, if your product is a computer or a copier machine, you may want to offer a loaner until the customer's order is delivered. The use of a loaner keeps the buyer committed to owning the product. After the customer sees how much easier her life is because of your product, she won't even consider being without one. And if there are a few bugs to be worked out on your agreement or delivery of the product, the buyers who have a loaner in their possession are more likely to continue to own, despite any complications.

Delivering what you promise — and fast

Never, ever make promises that you aren't positive you can keep. If you close the sale by making unrealistic promises, you may find the product right back in your lap. When you don't live up to your promise, you fall from exceptional status to below standard performance: You aren't a person who just happened to make a mistake — you're a liar. Don't allow yourself to fall into the trap of making promises you can't keep — you may lose the sale you thought you had. If you have a history with this customer, you may be able to ride on past performance, but if this is the first time you've done business with this particular customer, it will probably be your last!

Silence is golden

Keeping your mouth shut is much easier said than done. After you've made a successful close, get the paperwork authorized and get out of their face. The more you talk after the customer says yes, the more possibilities you create to talk yourself right out of a sale.

Before you're tempted to make conversation after the customer says yes to owning your product or service, think about the danger of bringing up something she hadn't thought about that may prevent her from going ahead with the purchase. You may inadvertently introduce new doubts and concerns that she hadn't even thought of. Excited prattle by a salesperson often leads to the reopening of the selling situation. This may sound mean, but when you get a yes, it's time to shut up. Without appearing too eager, pack up your briefcase and beat a path to the door with your authorization for ownership. As much as people dwell on things and sweat the details of making decisions, once the decision is made, they're as ready to move on as you are.

Beefing up your follow-up

If your challenge isn't in closing the sale, but rather in keeping the sale closed, you need to take a personal inventory of what you may or may not be doing to reinforce strong positive feelings regarding ownership of your product or service. If you find yourself negotiating a sale two and three times before closing and then successfully keeping the sale closed, you need to identify your weaknesses and do what it takes to strengthen those areas of improvement. Here are some things to keep in mind:

✔ Do you send your thank-you notes within 24 hours of closing the sale?

✔ Do you follow up to confirm the delivery date or start-up date?

✔ Are you making a quick satisfaction call or visit within 30 days of ownership?

In other words, are you providing the service and attention the customer needs? If not, beef up your follow-up program today.

Lastly, keeping the sale closed means keeping the relationship open. Always be honest and show your integrity; this will make the customers feel comfortable enough to come to you when they haven't received what they consider to be fair service or attention to their needs. If you haven't established this sort of relationship, you may end up dealing with after-the-sale objections or having to negotiate the sale several times before a successful close, and your long-term business relationships will be almost nonexistent. When this happens, you'll be working twice as hard to do half the business. Keep the sale closed by keeping an ongoing relationship with past customers, who will, in turn, be ambassadors of your future business.

Add-On Selling

*T*he time will come for you to go beyond the close and move on to add-on sales. Too many salespeople make a sale and begin thinking of moving on to the next client — they don't think of the additional items and services they could offer this client. Think of add-on selling in terms of building: You're closing the original sale, but building your relationship with the client toward future business.

Unless you market a single, one-time-only, non-consumable product, you need to master the skills of adding on to your first sale with every client. For example, if you sell insurance, would you consider your work done with clients after they got involved with one whole life policy? Of course not. You'd attempt to insure their home, their cars, boats, motorcycles, children, jewelry, and cabin in the mountains, wouldn't you? Even if you do sell a one-time-only product, your client may like it well enough to get a second one as a gift for someone else. Get the picture? You should never consider the sale complete with just one item.

Mastering the Add-On Sale

After the buying impulse starts and the doors have been opened by the first sale, your customers are very susceptible to purchasing another product you represent. Momemtum is working in your favor, which is why add-ons are usually a much quicker sell. After all, the customers already like you, trust you, and know the quality of products your company produces. The thing to keep in mind is that whenever you think you're finished with a sale, you're probably not. After the first close, approximately 15 percent of clients commit to add-ons. All it takes is persistence, patience, skill, timing, and product knowledge.

Look at add-on selling as a way to build a long-lasting relationship of continued trust and respect with each new client. As part of this relationship, you serve the customers' needs as they arise, thus increasing your sales. This is what add-on selling is all about, and it can increase your sales volume by 25 to 50 percent. But before you rush out and go add-on crazy, you have to perfect your method.

Becoming product proficient

In the beginning of your sales career, becoming an expert on a few items may be better than trying to learn them all and knowing none of the products very well. However, after you master the features of a few products, don't stop there. In order to master add-on selling, you have to know your product line inside and out. Even though there may be one or two particular favorites you like to sell, you limit yourself and your clients' potential success when you present only your favorites to them. Make an effort to learn how the products your company manufactures link to one another. Not only will you add the new products to your professional repertoire, you'll also be able to successfully add them on to original sales. As you get to know the customers' needs in your first selling cycle with them, constantly keep in mind other products that tie in with the product they're currently considering.

Keep in mind that your success at add-on selling is better when the products are related and complement one another. For example, if your customer owns one of your computers, a logical add-on item may be additional RAM or an external hard drive.

When you are constantly seeking out add-on opportunities, you learn more and more about your products and what they can do for your clients. The knowledge you gain will in turn earn you more and more.

Don't determine the add-ons you offer your customers based on bonuses you'll receive. The customer will see right through your ulterior motive and walk out the door. In other words, if your company is offering special bonuses to salespeople who sell the most phone systems and you can't link the phone system to a customer's previous purchase, don't present the add-on and take the chance on losing a good customer. If customers feel used, they're going to give you the boot.

Think "big picture"

Practicing add-on selling requires you to have vision. See and sell the big picture! The only thing that limits the number of add-ons you can sell to each client is your own imagination or creativity. Every sales professional gets the chance to offer more and to increase his/her income as well as the customers' satisfaction. A good example of the big picture is found in the restaurant business. Appetizers and desserts are considered add-ons. Servers are paid additional bonuses and earn company perks based on the number of add-ons they persuade their customers to enjoy. If you have a well-trained server, rarely will you leave a restaurant without at least one add-on to your ticket. The best servers always assume you've come in for the entire dinner experience, not just for a quick entree. Servers know that it doesn't take many of these add-ons to qualify for bonuses, not to mention a bigger tip.

Before you present the big picture, you need to first close on the original item the customers came to buy; then describe the big picture. For example, say you're dealing with a couple who just purchased a swimming pool. After the close, help them envision themselves enjoying the pool by adding to the picture. Mention a built-in barbecue where the customers can grill mouthwatering steaks and also a water volleyball set that will provide hours of fun exercise in the sparkling pool. Of course, an additional pool deck should be added to complete the beauty of this backyard paradise, not to mention a wonderful patio set that offers outdoor dining at its best.

What have you created with this picture? Elevated emotion! Instead of just plopping a pool somewhere in the backyard, you've given the big picture to your customers. They see themselves sitting out by the pool. They smell the steaks smoking on the grill. They imagine the enjoyment their whole family can have playing water volleyball. They hear the sounds of laughter and excitement as one side scores against the other. They feel the deck beneath their bare feet. By offering all these additional add-ons, you give your customers the opportunity (and incentive) to enjoy the whole enchilada!

You're the expert

As a sales professional, learning the ins and outs of your product or service is critical. With in-depth study of the industry and your product knowledge, you come across as an expert in your field. Take advantage of that expert status by making "expert recommendations."

Here's an example of expert add-on selling:

I appreciate your letting me market your property. Statistics have indicated that pre-owned homes sell quicker and for more money if they have a one-year home warranty on them. I know you're not interested in taking care of the house after closing; however, challenges may arise after the new owners have moved in. Wouldn't you agree that $350 is not much to invest for peace of mind and to prevent the possibility that you may face an unpleasant situation later?

The dialogue above is effective because the salesperson presents himself as the qualified expert. When making purchasing decisions, the advice from the salesperson can be extremely helpful. As their professional expert, your customers trust you to point them in the right direction with their best interest in mind. Look at add-ons as your opportunity to show your expertise.

Keep your eyes on the solution to the customers' challenges instead of on their pocketbook. In the long run, you'll achieve a much longer-lasting relationship and greater sales opportunities with each client.

You want fries with that?

Because selling is a hobby of mine, I always pay attention to good service and salesmanship skills anywhere I go. Restaurant servers are especially easy to observe when you're the client. I make mental notes of how much my wife, guests, and I enjoy ourselves, and how much more we end up adding to our dinners when we have an exceptional server. I have been fortunate to have the opportunity to train servers and managers of the Big Four restaurant chain in my hometown of Phoenix, Arizona. Instead of asking if the customer would like a drink while reviewing the menu, I taught the servers to ask, "Shall I bring you a soda, glass of wine, or a mixed drink?" Minor change, big difference. Some of the other material I had them say included: "How many slices of our fresh apple pie shall I bring for you?" and "We have an excellent dessert wine that complements the cheesecake perfectly. I'll be happy to bring it with your dessert." People are in the restaurant to eat, so why not make their dining experience bigger and better?

Accessorize, accessorize, accessorize!

Typically, add-ons don't involve a whole other line of products; add-ons usually mean your customers take a second look at the product they currently use in search of ways to make the product more efficient and cost effective. Instead of an entirely different product, they may just need an accessory or an attachment to enhance the product they already own. In fact, add-ons can actually save your customers money. Rather than purchasing another product, the customers are saving money by upgrading and/or enhancing their existing product. In the words of any number of fashion moguls, it's all in the accessories, baby.

Expanding your options

If you are servicing a large account and you communicate primarily with only one department head, expand your thinking. Will your product or service benefit another department of the same company? What could you sell as add-ons if you were to meet with other department heads and discover their needs as well? Use your present contact person to meet other potential clients. Here's an effective way to ask your contact person for this information:

> You mentioned working interactively with the manufacturing department. Who makes the decisions on the copier needs?

After you get the name, have your contact introduce you to the proper person. In many companies, each department is like its own kingdom and an introduction is all that's needed to open the door for further discussions.

In dealing with more than one department, you may come across a cooperative selling opportunity where a portion of each department's budget is contributed to owning your product. Cooperative selling opportunities are handy, especially if what you're offering costs more than one department can afford. When this is the case, the potential add-ons presented may need to be department specific. By that I mean one department in a company may have a particular add-on as a *primary need* while it's a *luxury* for another department. Because the first department really needs it, the second will be gung ho for this great feature as well, and you can frequently add up to a 50 percent increase in your sales volume.

Asking the Big Question

Some salespeople think they're doing great if they can get the sale in the first place, which makes them feel they're asking too much if they start adding on. If this is the way you feel, then don't try to add on sales. But realize that you're missing out on some tremendous opportunities for additional business, and you may even be doing a disservice to some of your clients who wonder why you didn't offer them the added benefits.

When it comes to add-on sales, the customer's already in the buying mode. Oftentimes, the add-ons are what create the excitement in the sale. Think of car sales. Sure, your customers could own a stripped, for-transportation-only model, and the car would get them from one location to another. However, if the customers added fancy wheels, four-wheel-drive capabilities, leather interior, an unbelievable stereo, and reinforced bumpers for towing and pulling, they would feel much differently about driving the vehicle. Suddenly driving would be a pleasant experience instead of a chore! They wouldn't have just transportation and a way to get around; they would own a multi-purpose vehicle. They would achieve a higher status level. They would have more pride when showing it off to neighbors, friends, and relatives. Add-ons can make the car deal a whole different ball game.

Think of add-on selling as offering additional benefits, and you won't have to justify the reasons for add-on selling.

With add-on selling, you need to maintain an assumptive attitude. If your client is investing in a copier, it's only natural to assume he'll want an extended warranty. And what about toner for the machine? Are you also able to provide copier paper at an economic price? The client will need all these things, so why not assume you'll be the one providing them?

Timing is everything

Timing is everything when it comes to add-on sales. If you've just convinced a customer to stretch his budget to the max by owning your most expensive and highest-performing product, now may not be the time to offer an add-on. Tension may be high and the customer probably needs time to let the purchase sink in. Let the pressure wear down a little. Waiting doesn't mean you'll never offer the customer an add-on; it just means that today isn't the time.

Like a good comedian who knows the importance of timing, wait for the right moment. Comedians have the timing thing down to a science. In addition to practicing telling a joke, they also perfect their delivery. Comedians combine a joke with other jokes, add proper pauses and meaningful looks, and above all, practice timing. Use the same tactic when offering add-ons. If you want the standing ovation, you sometimes have to wait for it; build the momentum and create an atmosphere of expectation first. The following conversation shows good timing on the part of the salesperson:

CHAMPION STRATEGY

You: I'm so happy you've decided to own an ABC microwave. You're going to be thrilled with the time you'll save. You'll be able to prepare a complete meal in the time it used to take you to simply think it over!

Them: I can't wait! Can I bake in it as well?

You: Are you a baker? Oh, you're going to love the feature ABC just came out with for confectionery cooking! The feature is very new. It's a carousel that provides even baking and easy-to-accomplish gourmet results! Wait until you get a look at this! For just a few dollars more, your new microwave can be your right hand assistant for baking as well as preparing the main dishes.

Them: Well, I don't know. We just spent $50 over what we originally planned to on this microwave.

You: I totally understand, but while you're here, why don't you take a look at it — you'll have a new item for your Christmas list! ABC just put this feature on the market, so I'm sure they'll still be offering it when you're ready to own. In fact, if it's something you'd be interested in, I'll be happy to give you a call when it goes on sale. Take a look at this — you won't believe it!

In this example, the salesperson knew of the add-on but didn't try to sell it initially. The clients has already agreed to invest more than they originally planned, so the salesperson waited for their cue as to what additional features they wanted before bringing up another feature.

Follow this one fundamental rule for add-on sales: Never go for the add-on sale until you've completely closed the original sale! Put yourself in the place of your customer. For example, say you needed a vacuum cleaner and went to an appliance store. Would you want the salesperson to start telling you about a fantastic new microwave that lets you prepare your food in half the time? Of course not. What you want to hear about is a vacuum cleaner. If the salesperson kept talking about the microwave, not only would he never close you on a vacuum cleaner, but he'd lose out on the microwave sale as well — and potentially lose out on any future business with you.

The key to add-on selling is to satisfy one need before moving to another. Don't rush the add-on sale.

Leading the horse to water

When you're ready to ask for the add-on, your questioning strategies and techniques play a vital role. (I cover questioning strategies and techniques in detail in Chapter 5.) You must master your questioning tactics to become a master of add-on sales. You already know the customer needs your original offering; now you're listening for add-on requests. Continuing to ask questions is how you find out what the customer's additional needs are for future or immediate add-on sales. Through insightful questioning strategies and practices, you can link one product to another, and both you and your customer will benefit. Following are a few questioning tactics to keep in mind:

✔ Use tie downs to build the "yes" momentum.

A tie down is usually an "isn't that right?" question at the end of sentence that calls for some sort of agreement from the listener. (For more on using tie downs, take a look at Chapter 5.)

> Having a neutral color in your carpeting is important to you, isn't it?

✔ Use leading questions to guide the selling process in the direction you want it to go.

For example, if they haven't yet discussed replacing their carpet padding, you can ask:

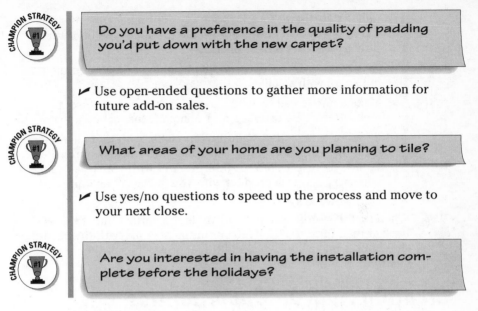

Do you have a preference in the quality of padding you'd put down with the new carpet?

✔ Use open-ended questions to gather more information for future add-on sales.

What areas of your home are you planning to tile?

✔ Use yes/no questions to speed up the process and move to your next close.

Are you interested in having the installation complete before the holidays?

Before you know it, your add-ons can amount to as much as, if not more than, the original purchase. All you have to do is ask — and use the right question.

Getting back in touch

After a customer has said yes to you and your product, he's much more likely to want to repeat the performance — you just need to figure out when and how. You may choose to sell add-ons directly after the close of your original offering, during that same visit. Or you may want to give the customer a little breathing space and wait to contact him again. (See the section "Timing is everything" in this chapter for more on the waiting game.) Maybe an FYI (For Your Information) call can be made to inform the customer of an additional product that perfectly complements the one he already owns.

If you decide that it's best to wait awhile before talking to the customer about add-ons, knowing how to get back in contact with customers when the time comes is one of the biggest challenges many salespeople face. There are several ways to re-establish contact, which the following list shows:

✔ Call the customer to let him know you're there to serve his needs — and then add an "Oh, by the way. . ." to lead into another product or service.

✔ Call the customer to ask about any additional concerns he has as a way to mention additional products you offer that directly address those concerns.

✔ Fax the customer a new products catalog or flyer and then follow up with a call.

✔ Make a phone call to say hello and talk about your excitement over a new product your company just came out with.

✔ If you've established a good relationship with that customer, drop by to check on how he's doing with his new purchase. While you're at it, bring a new product with you. (Make sure you carry an extra product with you in case of an immediate sale.)

When you're re-contacting the client is the perfect time to look back at the notes you took in your initial meeting with the client; these notes may show what additional products suit the customer's future needs.

Creating Add-On Opportunities

Like any other selling strategy, there are several things the salesperson can do to create — and maintain — add-on sales opportunities. Some of the ways to do this include:

✔ **Looking for buying potential.** What is the buying potential of your customers? How much can they afford now and in the future? Did the customers mention what they plan to do with their upcoming tax refund? Look for the best time to present add-on items by finding out when the customers will be able to finance. Remember, the more you enable the customer to grow his business using your products, the more chance you have to grow your business as well.

✔ **Discussing other concerns.** What other concerns do the customers have now that they've invested in one of the products? Do you have a product that complements the one they now own? Is there a way to increase their vision by increasing your offerings? Ask "What would you think if we could. . . ." and then mention a potential added benefit you can provide.

✔ **Constantly relieving the pressure of closing.** When you make the sale, it's common for your customers to experience some degree of pressure — that's what selling is all about. When salespeople successfully sell, it's usually because they were able to relieve the pressure a client felt about making a decision. Any time you're influencing

another to make a decision he may not have otherwise
made, you're building pressure. Here are some phrases you
can use to diminish the pressure when you enter an add-on
selling situation:

> I know you may not really be ready. . . .
>
> I hope you don't think I'm being pushy, but. . . .
>
> I know you may not be interested at this point, but. . . .
>
> Not to make assumptions, but. . . .

Add-ons should be no pressure, just continued excitement. If the
customer feels pressured in any way, take the pressure off. Leave
the add-on for another time.

The keys to success with add-on selling are to keep your eyes
and ears open to any additional needs your client may have and
to know all the possible add-on items that you have available
to them.

The Possibilities Are Endless

Some products have options and features that are not part of the
standard package but can be added on — and your customers
want to know about them. As an example, how many people do
you think really want to own a new car with no air conditioning,
no radio, and plain old vinyl seat covers? I called a local car
dealership the other day and was told that they won't even put a
basic, no-frills car on the lot. Everyone wants the extras, so be
sure to offer them.

Many tangible products such a cars, appliances, and office
equipment come with extended warranties as available add-ons.

For another example of easy add-on selling, consider the furniture business. Furniture salespeople are excellent at add-on
business. Rarely does a customer walk away with only the one
item he intended on purchasing. When was the last time you
purchased a living room sofa and didn't come away with at least
two or three additional items? Of course, it starts with the sofa
the customer originally comes in to the store to buy. Next comes
the can of fabric treatment. Then comes one or two decorator
pillows, a couple of new end table lamps to update the living

room's look, and so on. The add-ons are practically endless, and not just in the furniture business. As I say earlier in the chapter, you can find an add-on for just about any product.

The element of surprise

A young man who used to work for our company is now in the furniture business. A woman who had purchased a new home came into his store and was looking for living room furniture. She wanted to start with just a sofa and maybe a chair. He determined her taste in furniture and the style that suited her needs. Her plan was to acquire a few pieces at a time to keep the decorating within her budget. Of course, during the process, she commented on various additional pieces that she thought would look great and expressed excitement at having the whole ensemble a few months down the road.

After completion of the sale, a delivery time was arranged. My young friend did his homework on the investment for the entire suite she had favored, determined that she could afford the suite with the discounts he could offer on the larger purchase, and had his delivery people load up everything: sofa, love seat, chair,

tables, lamps, artwork for the walls, and various knickknacks. He went along with them to make the delivery. The young man asked the customer to show him the room and where she'd like the sofa placed. Then, he asked her to leave the room while they moved it in.

Within 20 minutes, he had transformed her empty living room into the living room of her dreams. When she walked in, she was speechless. He told her that he knew she hadn't committed to all the pieces he brought with him, but he wanted her to see the full effect of everything she had shown interest in. After he saw that she was emotionally involved in the results, he explained the reduced investment he was able to offer on the entire room full of furniture. She gladly agreed to having him leave the whole package. There was no way she wanted to see a half-empty room again!

Chapter 12

Bowing Out Gracefully (But Keeping Your Foot in the Door!)

In This Chapter

▶ Leaving a good impression

▶ Going for referrals

▶ Keeping in touch with clients

▶ Maintaining relationships

▶ Analyzing what went wrong

▶ Setting aside your pride

▶ Increasing your skill level

▶ Saying good-bye the right way at the right time

*J*ust as a sale doesn't end with the close when you *do* get the business, it also doesn't end with the close when you *don't* get the business. The close is the opening of a relationship — just because the prospective customer doesn't own your product or service doesn't mean she doesn't offer potential for future business. A person who doesn't buy from you is still a prospect; it's up to you to continue to romance the customer into saying "Yes!" next time.

Sell Yourself (With a Mind toward Future Sales)

The day you bow out of a sale may be one of your last opportunities to speak with a particular prospect. So, make the meeting worth their time and yours. How?

✔ Continue to entice them — sell them on your company and your product or service.

✔ Sell yourself — your expertise and your personal dedication to service.

✔ Make the prospective customers feel good about having met you so that they look for a way to give you some business, even if it isn't at the level you expected.

Champion salespeople know how to turn that foot in the door into a full-blown account by providing their customers excellent service and quality product on the little things — thus earning their business on the bigger things.

Here's an example of what you can say after your prospective customer has informed you that she has decided to go with your competition:

Them:	I really hate to tell you this, but we've decided to go with ABC Company. Thanks for all the time you spent with us, though!
You:	I'm glad for you that you've made your decision and that I had this opportunity to meet you and show you our product. So you think ABC Company has more to offer you in the way of product and service?
Them:	It really boiled down to a matter of price. We have such a tight budget this year. I appreciate your efforts to give us the best price, but it just wasn't low enough.
You:	I understand. Let me ask you a question. Because I pride myself on the business relationships I've worked hard to maintain over the years — and I feel we communicated quite well — would you mind if I just popped in sometime during the next month or two to see how you're getting along with the new equipment?
Them:	Sure, that would be okay.
You:	I can't say that I'm not sorry to have lost your business this time, but maybe there will be something I can help you with in the future. I'm sure your decision came after much examination of all the products and services presented to you. If you're like the rest of us, though, sometimes you're unable to make the best choice based on the limited amount of information and knowledge you have at the time, wouldn't you agree?

> **Them:** I've made my share of mistakes, that's for sure!
>
> **You:** I hope this isn't one of them, but if it is, will you promise me one thing? Will you promise me that you'll call me if there is anything I can do to help? Does that sound agreeable?
>
> **Them:** Sure, that's fine.
>
> **You:** Okay, I'll see you later. Best of luck to you and your company in owning your new equipment!

This conversation warrants an examination. In the following list, I go through some elements of the conversation so you can see just what was achieved and how the salesperson bowed out gracefully but left his foot in the door for future business.

✔ The customer is feeling a bit guilty for going with your competition, especially after you spent a lot of time with her and educated her about your product or service. Chances are, you're disappointed, too! Showing your disappointment is okay, but be sure to stay composed and professional. Maintaining composure may take some practice. (Unfortunately, it's a given in sales that you'll have plenty of opportunities for such practice!)

✔ Ask her for reasons why she chose your competition. Your question can be worded as simply as:

> So you think ABC Company had more to offer you in the way of product and service?

No pressure, no anger, just a matter-of-fact statement. You can also say:

> May I ask you, without being too presumptuous, what made you choose ABC Company over us?

If you put the fault on the company instead of the salesperson, the prospective customer won't feel as though she is saying something negative about you personally — and she's more likely to give you the true reason.

✔ Indicate that you take great pride in the business relationships you've created throughout your years as a representative for XYZ Company and that you would like to know if it was anything you said or did that swayed her to go with the competition. If she says you were very professional, ask for some referrals.

✔ Did you notice the part about popping in to see how she's getting along? This is a great, no-pressure way to ask permission to see her again. When asking a customer if you can stop by, make sure you put the date way out in the future somewhere. (Not that you actually have to wait an entire month or two; you can pop in a little sooner, don't you think?) When you do stop by, approach the receptionist or secretary with something like this:

> Hi, my name is (your name here) and (your client's name here) asked me to pop in for a quick one- or two-minute meeting. Would you let her know I'm here, please?

Obviously, this "pop in" method won't work for every situation, but why not use it on those occasions when it does?

✔ Notice how the salesperson complimented the customer on her ability to make decisions, but left the door open for her to contact him in case this particular decision wasn't the best one to make at the time. He got the customer to admit she had made mistakes when deciding things in the past, and then he offered to help her out with any questions she may have. In fact, he almost got a formal agreement.

✔ Wish your client good luck on owning her new product or service to show your good will.

Through this one conversation, the salesperson was able to leave a favorable impression and didn't make the customer feel uncomfortable about letting him down. He was able to keep his foot in the door for future business by offering to assist her with any questions she may have or information she may need. He made her feel good by paying her a little compliment, yet created the slightest of questions in her mind. And then he made her feel okay about (perhaps) making a mistake, because he will be there to help her out.

Copying the copier closer

I know a young man in copier sales who has had a solid connection with my company for many years. The initial relationship was one in which we chose the competition over his product, but he stuck with us. Later, when we needed to upgrade our copier, he was representing the best copier for our needs. We did become his client — and was his service ever exceptional!

Our next purchase of a copier took us away from him again. He just didn't have the product we needed at the investment we were willing to make. But, guess what? He still stops by every now and then. He says hello to the staff (who, of course, remember him because of his excellent service). He checks the copy volume on our current machine and asks about our needs. One day he even changed the toner for us on a competitor's machine! Who do you think we'll call first when that machine needs to be replaced?

After you've sold yourself to the customer, don't just sit back, waiting and hoping for the best. Keep in touch with the prospect because that's what the customer still is — a prospect. Most top producers can tell you stories of prospects who contacted them and asked them to come in and do a presentation on their product or service a year or more after the producer thought the sale was lost forever to competitors. Show the customer how well you service an account that isn't even yours yet, and she'll link your name and product or service with quality and caring attention to her needs.

Ask for Referrals

Another great way to benefit from a non-sale is to at least go for referrals. Try this:

CHAMPION STRATEGY #1

> Were you at least happy with the way I handled the research and presentation of our solution?

In most cases, the customer will say yes because she doesn't want to beat you up any more than she already has. When she agrees that you're a good person and did a good job, that's the time to ask for referrals.

> Well, then, you wouldn't mind referring others to me who have needs similar to yours, would you? Our product may be right for them.

Most of the time the unclient will agree. Now you simply hand her three of your business cards and say:

> You can rest assured that anyone you refer to me will be treated with the same quality of service I've demonstrated with you. I look forward to hearing from them and will let you know the outcome of any business your referral generates.

You've just jammed a big rock in that doorway, keeping it open for the future. You *have* to stay in touch with her now to get referrals and report back to her. With each contact, you nudge that door open just a little more toward future business with her.

Continue to Communicate with Your Client

Keep yourself and your company name in front of the customer's face at all times. Learn to communicate with the client in different ways, too. Almost every salesperson relies on the telephone to keep in touch, so be creative — be different. Sure you'll want to call every now and then, but do something a little out of the norm so the customer remembers you.

- ✔ After you lose a potential client's business, send her a thank-you note and congratulate her on making a decision to grow. Tell the prospect how much you appreciated the opportunity to meet with her and that you'll be in touch.

- ✔ I discuss the power of thank-you notes in-depth in *Selling For Dummies.* Here's the best one for this particular situation.

> Thank you for taking the time to analyze my services. I regret being unable to help you appreciate the benefits that we can provide you at this time. We keep constantly informed of new developments and changes in our industry, though, so I'll keep in touch with you in the hope that, in the years ahead, we may be able to do business.

✔ Look back at the notes you took from your meeting where the customer may have mentioned some special challenges she was having, and then fax her newspaper or magazine articles that address the challenges. By providing this courtesy, you let your prospect know that you're thinking of her, and it also shows her the new light you can shed on her current situation.

✔ Another great form of communicating is through e-mail. Sending an e-mail makes the recipient feel that the message is something personal, private — even urgent. The prospect can read an e-mail at her convenience and focus on your message. And if there was a little joke you both shared, remind her of it in the e-mail message. Perhaps you had a lot in common. Reinforce that bond in the message you send.

E-mail gives immediacy to the message, which prompts the client to read the message. E-mail can be a powerful tool, which is why it's so important during the selling process to get the prospect's fax number and e-mail address. Keep in mind that e-mail gives you options on methods of communication that other salespeople may not think to consider. (For more on communicating with e-mail, see Chapter 9.)

When you show the prospect that you care and that she means more to you than just a fee for service, you earn the right to continue communicating with her. Keep the client informed of your company's latest improved product or service and make her feel special by being the "first to know."

Keep Talking to Other Folks, Too

One way to assertively hold the inside track with a client is to maintain those third-party relationships that helped you get your foot in the door in the first place. Send thank-you cards to the receptionist, secretary, and assistant of the client's company in addition to the client herself. Show these third-party people that you appreciate all of their efforts that first created the opportunity for you to make the initial contact. Let them know that you think their company is lucky to have them and that their input is very important to you.

Giving this special attention to the third-party people pays off when you make your follow-up calls. If the decision maker is not available, chances are pretty good that one of these well-appreciated-by-you people will have a moment to chat with you about everyone's thoughts and feelings on the new equipment and service that the competition is providing. In fact, you may get better background information from these people than from the decision maker, so keep these doors and windows of opportunity open!

Forever is a long, long time

Forever is a long, long time, so why would you think losing the business this one time means never doing business with the customer again? Who knows — the customer may recognize her mistake and appreciate you popping in a short while down the road. Or maybe the decision maker will change positions, and the new contact will be ready to make some dramatic changes in how things are currently being done. Or perhaps your competitor made a lot of promises the company can't fulfill. Now it's your turn to step in and show what you and your company can do.

Keep this in mind: When your customer or prospect decides to go with your competitor, don't take it personally, and don't make it a personal issue with the customer, either. Being told no was a temporary setback, but it doesn't mean forever! "No" just means "not now." By asking your client why she chose to go with your competition, you are receiving some valuable information that will help you in your next contact with her. And when that times comes, you definitely have the upper hand because you know just what it was that convinced her to make a decision the first time. People may change products or services, but when it comes to communicating with people, they usually remain consistent in their behavior.

ANECDOTE

Turning a negative into a positive

A young woman once left her son at a daycare center and promised the tearful child she'd be back to pick him up at 5:00 sharp. Sure enough, when she showed up at 5:00 p.m. there was no young man in sight. As she quickly stepped out of her car, she saw the daycare director leading her bandaged son out to her. The child's face was pale, his expression serious, and his step a little slower — until his little friend came running out to say good-bye. When asked what happened, the daycare director stated that her son had been pushed from behind while standing in the lunch line by this same little boy who came out to say good-bye. The mother turned to her son and said, "Well, I guess you won't be playing with that young man any more, will you darling?" Her son replied, "No, mom. We got to be friends after that! I think I'll just have to be last in line from now on!"

We can all learn an important lesson from this little boy. Don't cut the relationship just because you're rejected or hurt. Find another way to make it positive and enjoy doing business with that person. Turn the negative into a positive! After all, if a five-year-old can do it, so can you.

Analyze the Lost Sale

After doing the best you can, realize that the relationship has come to a close (for now) and that it's time to cut your losses and move on. Don't put this negative experience out of your mind, though; learn from it. Make this experience your teacher in the next transaction you enter. Make the negative experience your friend, your companion in that next meeting. Remember what went wrong and vow not to repeat the performance. After you've reviewed the negative events in the sale, say "next" and move on to the positive feelings you're determined to create in the next and all other sales relationships.

Many educators will tell you to put the negative right out of your head — but how do you learn from the experience if you choose to ignore it? Since childhood we are taught by the negative experiences as well as the positive ones. In fact, some of those negative experiences are much more memorable than the positive ones. If you burn your hand on a hot stove, you learn not to touch the burner when it's red. If you fail in one area, and then compensate for that failure, you learn that one failure does not mean failure overall.

Conduct the dead sale autopsy

The time has come to do what I call *dead sale autopsy:* examining what went wrong and finding solutions to make it right. If the sale is dead, you have to figure out what caused the disease, what made it spread, and then commit to making the next contact a healthy one. This learning process won't always be pleasant — sometimes it downright stinks. But if you're determined to make the best of a dead sale, you have to break down its parts and see what went wrong. Start by calling the decision maker:

I know you've decided to go with another company on this decision. Again, I want you to know that I really appreciate having had the opportunity to meet with you and present my product. I'm sincerely happy that you're satisfied with your decision on this purchase and hope that you'll at least consider doing business with us sometime in the future. In fact, I have a little something I'd like to bring by to thank you for the time we shared. It will just take me a few moments to drop it off. Is 3:15 okay, or would it be better if I wait until just before 5:00?

You'll encounter people who refuse to meet with you again. For those who refuse, offer the alternative of sending a brief survey they could fax back to you. If they refuse this as well, thank them again for their time and consideration of your product and try to get permission to send them future information of advances in the technology of the industry or improvements in your service.

For those who agree to this brief visit, be prepared with an appropriate gift and use these words:

> I want you to know how much I appreciate the time you spent considering our company for your recent purchase. Here is a small token of my appreciation. I was wondering if I may ask you just a couple of questions to clarify my understanding of your decision?

Ask these questions:

- ✔ Were there any areas of miscommunication?
- ✔ Did you receive information in an easy-to-understand manner?
- ✔ Was all the information you needed provided? Did the competition provide anything additional that helped you make your decision?
- ✔ What were the benefits that made you choose the other company?
- ✔ Is there anything I could have done better in my presentation that may have swayed you to our company?

If she hesitates at all, say:

> Please give me your honest opinion — don't worry about hurting my ego. I'm a professional. The information you give me may help me make another sale or help our company do better in the marketplace. My goal is to learn as much as possible from each contact I make — sale or no sale.

If your client still has some hesitation, you may want to persuade her further with:

> I'm sure your company would like having the same kind of information on sales not made, wouldn't it?

Take great notes on everything the client says. Consider every answer to be another bullet in your arsenal of selling skills. You're not only gaining information, you're also demonstrating how competent a salesperson you really are — and that's always the right impression to leave.

Evaluate your own behavior

Although it isn't the easiest thing to accept, it may be time to face the fact that perhaps you didn't deliver what you promised and therefore created bad feelings with your customers — and this may be the reason why they decided to change representatives or companies. If that is the case, if your customers have hard feelings because they feel they were treated poorly, don't let it go another day without confronting the situation head-on.

✔ Chances are if they felt that way, there was good reason, and you need to take a closer look at the cause of their concerns.

✔ Don't be afraid to apologize for a perceived wrongdoing, even if you believe yourself to be innocent. There is nothing like an apology to mend a damaged relationship. It's pretty difficult for someone to continue being angry when you go to them, face-to-face, and take responsibility for your behavior and ask them what it will take to right the wrong.

Don't suffer from the dreaded 3-11 rule!

The *3-11 rule* refers to the number of people your prospective client or new client will tell about you and your products and services. If your prospect or customer has a positive experience doing business with you, she's likely to tell approximately three people about it.

On the other hand, if she has a negative experience doing business with you, at least 11 others will hear about her unhappiness. The longer the wrong continues without any effort on your part to right it, the more people you give the client the opportunity to tell. Working in a large city with a huge customer base doesn't make you immune to the possibilities of a negative reputation preceding you. Don't risk it — ever!

When you truly keep what's best for the customers in mind, they can't help but notice and reward your efforts. Just as important, when their contact with you is positive, just think how many people they'll send to you. Make them all ambassadors of your business.

Set your pride aside

Although you need to be confident and competent, misplaced pride can cause you to lose a lot of business. If pride stands in the way of your apology or acceptance of defeat, it can cause you to damage your relationship with a potentially great client. And if pride keeps you from admitting that you don't know the answer, you may make a promise you can't deliver.

How long do you think it will take the customer to discover that you have more pride than principle? If pride keeps you from asking your prospect why she decided to go with your competitor, you may repeat the same mistakes over and over until you come to the decision that sales just isn't for you! True superstars don't have to pump up their pride; they are willing to admit their mistakes and turn them into memorable learning experiences.

What about you? Are you overcoming your pride? Think back on the last transaction that went sour. What did you do?

- ✔ Did you offer regret for not being able to fulfill their needs?
- ✔ Did you ask them why they went with your competitors?
- ✔ Did you keep in touch with them and show them you cared about the success of their company and not just that fat commission check you expected?
- ✔ Did you invest time sending them thank you notes and recognizing their secretary, assistant, or receptionist for their help?

Or did you let pride get in your way?

- ✔ Did you do like many other average salespeople and run out that door so fast that it couldn't close tight enough for your liking?
- ✔ Did you blame everybody and everything but yourself for your failure?

Now think about the very next meeting you had with a client. The residue from a perceived failure can be devastating to future selling situations. The sooner you realize that even the best of the best don't close every sale, the better off you'll be. Even top producers in your company create dissatisfaction in customers every now and then. And even the most unforgiving clients know when to continue a relationship with a representative who is trying to make amends and help them and their company to be more productive.

Increase your skill level

Chances are you were beat out of a sale because of a lack of skills and talents. So what do you do now? Well, you go back to the drawing board and increase your skill level.

- ✔ Look at what you did right and congratulate yourself on those things — even if it means starting with "I got out of bed this morning and I dressed professionally."
- ✔ Work your way through the day to the moment when you found out that you weren't getting the sale. Almost without fail, you find that being a weaker closer than the competition had something to do with the loss of that sale.
- ✔ Look at what you can improve and then do something about it.

Take responsibility for your lost sale, your inability to close. If you've lost to the competition, blaming your loss on everything or everybody else but yourself won't do you any good. Even if a successful close was beyond your capabilities with that particular customer, you still need to focus on improving your performance — and you will dramatically increase your sales. After you've taken a look at what you can do better, go out there and apply that knowledge. You may have lost the battle, but the war has just begun!

Finally, Know When to Say Good-bye

After keeping in close contact with a particular client for a reasonable time period — reasonable being a time period in which she should have had a need for your product — and you still haven't earned her business, it may be time to spread out the number of contacts you make with that prospect. I recommend you contact her not less than twice a year in order to keep your name fresh in her mind should a need arise, but more frequently than that may be a waste of your time and hers.

Part IV
The Part of Tens

The 5th Wave   By Rich Tennant

In this part...

*T*he quick tips and strategies found in this part are excellent material to review on your way to your next closing opportunity. These tips and tricks can help you adopt the proper closing mindset, allowing you to professionally assist your clients in making wise buying decisions.

Chapter 13

Ten Reasons People Choose Your Product or Service

. . . .

In This Chapter
▶ Understanding exactly why people want what you have to offer
▶ Using both logic and emotion to get customers involved

. . . .

*A*professional closer understands better than anyone that people don't always use logic when making ownership decisions; many times they make decisions based on emotion and then defend the decisions with logic. However, you may have cases where logic is the key element in the decision making. This chapter lists the top ten reasons, logical and emotional, why people decide on your particular product or service to serve their needs.

The Customer Wants Your Product

Yup. They want it. But it doesn't take a rocket scientist to figure out when a customer wants to make a purchase, so why do I mention it here? The reason why is because I've seen too many salespeople try to give people reasons to own something when it wasn't necessary — the customer's already convinced.

If someone comes into your store and tells you that he wants that new, high-tech pair of binoculars he saw reviewed in *Consumers Digest,* lead the customer to the display and encourage him in his interest, but don't be in too much of a hurry to get into the details of the product. The customer may not care. Just the fact that the binoculars got a high rating from *Consumers Digest* may be enough. If you start talking technical or asking the customer about how he'll use them, logic may set in — and the customer may talk himself right out of his "want." Instead, let the customer hold the binoculars — effectively taking ownership — and then gently lead the customer to the cash register.

The Customer Needs Your Product

You're bound to come across people who *need* your product but don't necessarily *want* it. For example, I have a friend who is in a position of needing a computer to perform certain complicated calculations and projections for his business. He, however, doesn't type, and he doesn't know a lot about computers, either. He just knows that a computer can fulfill his needs. At the same time, he feels somewhat forced into the technology by his need to keep up with the competition.

How do you handle this person? Well, the best thing to do is to keep things as simple as possible because there's plenty of room for Mr. Fear of Technology to participate in this selling scenario and cancel the whole thing. Concentrate on meeting the customer's particular needs without going overboard on all the other interesting things that he can do with this computer. Show how easy it is to master the software. Perhaps recommend a class that can teach him the basics.

People are always in need — and you need to ask the right questions to determine the whys behind their interest in your product or service. If someone needs a new car because their old one broke down, the sale is handled a bit differently than with someone who wants a new car just because their old one is old and they can make the purchase at their leisure. Recognizing the difference between these two customers and adjusting your sales approach accordingly will help you to close the sale.

Remember, a true professional can create such a strong desire for the customer to own that every reason to own becomes a need.

Your Product Is the Latest Version

If you sell computer hardware or software, you know how this one goes. As soon as there are rumors in the industry about a new version of something coming out, you'll be asked for it — even before anyone knows the difference between the new and old versions. This urgency is because people want to be the first to have the new version. The need to be first may be a status thing, a power trip, or a security issue. Whatever the reason, just be happy that manufacturers and developers continue to come out with new versions of everything.

I know a man who has to have the latest camera equipment. He isn't a professional photographer. In fact, he doesn't even take that many pictures. He just likes cameras and enjoys all the nifty features. His reasoning is that if he's going to take pictures, he wants the best quality picture he can possibly have — so he puts his faith in the new technology, even if he doesn't actually need or use the product.

Your Product Is the Biggest

This point applies to things like trucks, television sets, houses, and jewelry, where bigger is usually taken to mean better. This bigger-is-better mentality is often an ego thing, but don't scoff. Ego plays a very important part in every buying decision, so understand your customer's ego, and you can win with the right approach. Watch for the light of desire in the eyes of the beholder as they approach your product (it's easy to recognize the look). Capitalize on this opportunity by telling the customers how good your product will look to the neighbors, friends, or other sports fans. And don't forget to mention how great it will feel to be the ones who own the biggest on the block.

Your Product Is the Smallest

Here I'm talking high-tech. In the field of advanced technology, the smallest sized product makes the biggest splash. Mobile telephones started out weighing at least eight pounds and weren't all that mobile — and you had to have a car attached to them to make them work. Today's cellular phones are nearly as small as a credit card and offer crystal clear reception — and you don't need a car for them to work. Another example is with calculators. The challenge was to see how small and portable calculators could become. Well, my chief financial officer has one he wears as a watch. Talk about portable! And look at today's Walkman and Discman line of products — excellent quality in a compact size.

Also keep in mind that to some customers, smallest means simplest. Some people pride themselves on having just the basics because that's all they need. They don't want to own anything more than a simple AM/FM radio, and they want it to be small and portable — anything else would be extravagant.

Your Product Makes the Customer Feel Secure

Security is one of the most basic needs of all human beings. Everyone wants to feel secure. If you market a product that provides a feeling of security, use this angle in your close. This is ideal if you sell insurance: "Won't you sleep better tonight knowing that your children will be financially taken care of should anything happen to you?"

Appealing to a person's natural desire for security also works well with security products — whether the product you're selling is for the home, business, vehicle, or personal safety. Also, building credibility into your sales presentations and closes creates a sense of security and peace of mind for the customer.

Your Product Feeds the Customer's Vanity

People want to look good, in their own eyes and in the eyes of others. Looking good makes you feel good and it adds to your self-confidence.

Many health and beauty products fall into the vanity category; they're designed to make us look good both inside and out. Fitness equipment, health club memberships, and even cosmetic surgery can be vanity products. Sculptured nails and hairstyles are, too. If the product or service you provide will enhance, beautify, or repair damage to any aspect of someone's physical appearance, it's a vanity product for sure.

If you sell something that's individualized or customized, you're dealing with another vanity product. Take, for example, vanity license plates. Why are they called that if they don't enhance your car? Vanity plates are individualized because the person wants to stand out among the masses. When a person sports a vanity plate on their car, what he's saying is, "Hey, I'm witty. I'm special. I'm different."

Non-conformity is a form of vanity. If you sell something that's individualized or customized, vanity is the emotion to reckon with when closing the sale.

Be careful here in your interpretation of the word *vanity*. For many people, vanity has a negative connotation. In fact, if you look up vanity in the thesaurus, you find that it's synonymous with words like egotism, conceit, and pretension. However, you also find pride. People who are vain take pride in themselves, their appearance, and the appearance of the things they own; use this definition of vanity to close people on vanity products.

Your Product Brings Status

Face it. There are people in the world who think a Timex Ironman watch represents a certain status and then there are those who wouldn't be caught dead without their Rolexes. What the brand name is doesn't matter — if you market a product with a brand name (for example, ...*For Dummies* books), people will seek out you and your product because of their perceived image of what that brand name does for them.

I know people who won't consider wearing any jeans but Levi's and others who only purchase Wranglers. It's a matter of personal preference and what they think the label does for them. You won't know what your customer's particular hot button is for a product until you ask. After you know, use that knowledge when you close.

Your Product Is Appropriate for a Season or Event

In my hometown area of Phoenix, Arizona, I'd have to say a good portion of the population is enamored with our local sports teams, whether they're doing well or not. So many of us fans have invested, in varying degrees, in apparel with the logos of the Phoenix Suns, Cardinals, Rattlers, Coyotes, and Diamondbacks. And the sales of those items increase at the beginning of the season for each team, which it only makes sense.

Retailers start bringing out holiday items earlier and earlier each year (or so it seems). I know I saw Christmas decorations available in August this year at one of the craft stores, which is a boon for those crafters who plan ahead and create intricate projects for the holidays. (I myself just love Christmas. I have decorations for it in every room of my home.)

If you market something seasonal, you can't wait until the season is upon you to start selling: You have to build the anticipation. By building anticipation, you ensure that the customers will think of you when they're ready to make a purchase — even if it's not until the day before the event. Building emotions for big events like holidays, the Superbowl, and so on, is a fun way to make a living, so you have to *be* fun. Have a fun and helpful attitude, and your enthusiasm will be contagious.

The Customer Is Compulsive

As a salesperson, you gotta love compulsive shoppers. When you know you have someone in a buying mode, take advantage of the situation. For example, say you have a customer who just purchased new bed linens. Suggest that he take a look at your bathroom items. After all, who wants to admire a lovely bedroom and then see tacky, old towels in the bathroom?

Compulsion is an important emotional aspect of selling. Take, for example, the free demonstration food you find in grocery and warehouse stores. Compulsion is key here. The customer is already in the mindset to buy food, and by being offered a tasty morsel, the customer is compelled to buy even more food. You can apply this tactic no matter what product you sell.

Appealing to the quick decision maker (the compulsive shopper) is best for smaller-ticket items and add-ons — they won't invest a lot of time considering a small purchase. When adding on a sale, many people will be in the buying mode after they make major buying decisions and are receptive to enhancements for their new major purchases. An example of an add-on is fabric protection for sofas and chairs. (Check out Chapter 11 for more about add-on selling.)

Chapter 14

Ten Reasons People Don't Choose Your Product or Service

• •

In This Chapter

▶ Building trust and value

▶ Winning clients over

• •

I surveyed over 600 sales professionals to determine the most common reasons why people choose not to make a purchase. Believe me when I say that the salespeople had heard some pretty unusual responses from clients over the years; however, I did find that some reasons popped up over and over again. This chapter covers the most common ones.

Why am I giving you the ten reasons people don't buy? By knowing them ahead of time, you can have a response ready when the customer throws one out. And trust me, you will hear some of these.

Your Product Is Not the Best Product

I've started off with a tough one. If a client doesn't think that your product is the best one for her, you're challenged to call up all your selling skills — especially those you use in qualifying and determining the client's needs. Then, you need to muster your presentation skills to show the client exactly how your product does meet her needs (providing it actually does).

If, after some evaluation, you agree with the customer that your product is not the best one for her, bow out gracefully (check out Chapter 12 for some helpful ways to do this). If you act professionally with your client, even while bowing out, you create an opportunity for future business or referral business — even if you don't get the sale today.

Take note, though. If you hear this reason often — and you're losing to the competition quite frequently — you need to do some soul searching regarding your product. If you love your company or you're the owner of the company, you need to work on improving the quality or features of your product to stay competitive. If you represent a product and have no strong emotional attachment to the company, you may want to seriously consider representing a better product. The decision can be a tough one to make, but it's even tougher not having enough money to cover your living expenses.

Your Product Doesn't Stand Out

The fault here may lie with your marketing department. The responsibility of marketing is to make your product or service stand out as an individual among the masses. Your product has to shine brighter, taste better, look more high-tech, make you jump higher, run faster, or whatever. Your product can't be just like every other product or service in its category; if it is, your product won't sell like it should.

The Customer Procrastinates

Procrastination is certainly something that most of the world — not just your customers — has in common. But why do you think it is that so many customers procrastinate when making decisions? There are many reasons for this, but most of the time it's because of fear. Customers fear making a bad choice. They fear spending too much money. They fear losing face and committing professional hari-kari. Fear. Fear. Fear! (I cover several specific methods for overcoming buyer's fears in Chapter 6; Chapter 7 covers methods for facing down procrastination.)

Granted, if you're selling air fresheners for public rest rooms, you aren't as likely to encounter fear as you are if you're marketing high-end products and services, but all the same, there are people who are just simply afraid of making decisions. Your job is to ferret out the real reason behind the procrastination. Until you know what that reason is, making the sale is like trying to grab a handful of smoke — impossible. After you isolate the fear behind the procrastination, you can help the customer face her fear and overcome it — and you can close the sale.

The Customer Doesn't Want to Spend Money on Your Product

If money is the reason your customer's giving you for not making the purchase, it may mean she simply can't afford what she wants — she's the type of customer who has champagne tastes and a beer budget. Or maybe the customer has the money but is very frugal with it. Or perhaps you haven't given the customer enough reasons to believe that your product or service is worth her money. With excellent questioning skills (Chapter 5 helps you master those), you can determine which situation you're dealing with and move on from there.

If the situation is that the customer truly does not have enough money, be prepared to offer her a cut-rate product or service, leaving the door open to upgrading as she can. Or you can help your client find other sources for the money. In my real estate career, I was able to help many young families own their first homes even though they had small incomes. Through some discussion, we were often able to come up with a friend or relative who would give them a small loan to help them out. Or we discovered an insurance policy or other fund they could tap into that they hadn't previously considered as a source of money. And financing is a viable option as well. Many times people will find that they have better credit than they originally thought, making financing a possibility — and after they decide that they need your product, they're willing to pay the financing fees.

The Customer Doesn't Trust You or Your Product

If you've done everything by the book up to the closing point of a selling situation and people still don't buy from you, it may be that they don't trust you or that they don't trust that things will turn out the way you say they will. For this reason, I have taught my students for over 25 years that one of your first goals when you meet a person is to help that person like you, trust you, and therefore want to listen to you. You must position yourself as an expert in the industry or field you are representing. You must know your stuff and be willing and able to show them what you and your product can do — without becoming obnoxious about it.

If you impart an attitude of servitude in all of your business situations, you earn people's trust and confidence that what you have to offer will satisfy their needs.

The Customer Has Had a Bad Experience in the Past

You may not be aware of this, but generally speaking, salespeople are not highly thought of in most of the modern world. A negative stereotype is typically associated with people in the field of selling. If you're in doubt about this, notice how salespeople are portrayed in movies, television commercials, novels, and so on. I remember reading a newsletter a few years ago that said the job title of salesperson ranked just slightly above that of attorney in the United States on a list of least favorite people to have to deal with.

It's sad, but true, that many people have had bad past experiences with those who represent our field of work. Those who don't take selling seriously hurt our image. Those who use selling strategies to commit misdeeds hurt our image. And those who sell because of what's in it for them rather than what's in it for the customer kill many of our future chances with potential clients.

Patience is a necessity when dealing with a client you think may have had a bad experience in the past. Talk to the customer to find out what the previous experience was so you know exactly what you're up against. If the bad experience was product related and your product has changed since then, give a detailed explanation of the improvements. If the bad experience was with a representative of your product or service, point out that you're the one serving her now and then sell the customer on your personal competency. Bringing the customer back around may take more than one visit (if that's appropriate to the selling cycle of your particular product or service). You also may have to initiate several contacts including professional proposals, thank you notes, calls of concern to the customer to see how she's doing, and so on.

I compare dealing with a customer who's had a bad experience to building a new friendship. Your common ground is the product or service, but you need to show that you're interested in the other aspects of her business life as well. Establishing an attitude of being totally service-oriented goes a long way toward regaining trust and overcoming a bad past experience.

The Customer Is Indecisive

Over the course of a selling career, it is highly likely that you'll encounter people who just simply cannot make decisions. (Hopefully, you won't find too many of these people if you're working in business-to-business sales. An indecisive purchasing agent doesn't last long in that capacity.) However, if you make sales to the general populace, you're bound to find this type of customer.

Your goal with indecisive clients is to develop a strong enough desire for your product that they'll be afraid of the consequences of *not* having it. The key here is for you to deliver what you've promised as quickly as possible — before their indecision takes over again and they change their minds.

Sometimes humor works to crack the indecisive resolve of these people. Once they see the absurdity of some of the situations they've gotten themselves into, they'll loosen up and get down to the business of making a wise decision.

Your Timing Is Poor

It's gonna happen. You're going to contact a client to set up a meeting to present your product and find out that she made her purchase a week ago. Or maybe you get a lead for your telephone equipment and make contact the day the company decides to file for bankruptcy. Bad timing is inevitable. Face it, accept it, and then make the most of it. And always be professional. If you present yourself professionally, even if it's with bad timing, you can still make a good enough impression that you get referred business from the non-client. Referrals may not be the whole shootin' match of a sale, but it's a sale just the same.

Another option is to offer add-on services the other company couldn't provide. If someone buys a copier from another company, offer the best investment for toner or other supplies. How about service? Maybe your service agreement is the best in town. Does that mean you can sell it only to people who also invest in your product? Of course not. Be creative with bad timing situations. Always look for that silver lining. You'll be surprised at how often you find it.

The Customer Is Happy with Her Current Supplier

If the customer's happy with her current supplier, that's great for her — and you should tell her so. However, this should never be considered a dead end, even if the current supplier is a wholly-owned subsidiary of the customer's company — that is, the customer's company owns the supplier's company. It's a tough situation, but not impossible to overcome.

I had clients for whom I produced a sales training series. They were interested in only the video product because they owned a printing company and could get the printed matter (like workbooks and product packaging) created and printed on their own.

I said that was fine, but then asked if I could at least send them a proposal on how I handle that aspect of the business. They agreed just to be polite, never considering for a moment that they'd have me handle the printing. Well, to make the long story short, I not only beat the investment quoted by their in-house printing company, but also shortened the turnaround time by three weeks! Needless to say, I ended up providing the printing for them — and ten years later, I'm still fulfilling their training needs.

Whenever a customer tells you that she's happy with her current supplier, you need to become an investigator. Find out what made her choose that company. If you can match those determining factors, you've got a chance. Determine how long the customer has used her current supplier. If it's been a long time, you may have an advantage in that you've kept up with the times whereas the competing company has not. Service is another area to check. The other supplier may have become lazy in its servicing of the client — another door left open for you. Ask the client if you can at least give a comparison and be sure to point out that this is good information for the client to have to ensure that her regular supplier is still providing the best service possible. If you can raise even the slightest question in the mind of the buyer about whether or not you can do better than the current supplier, you're in the door. You will have earned the right to a presentation, or at the very least, a proposal.

You Never Asked the Customer for the Sale

Even though this was hard for our sales professionals to admit, they could all recount selling situations where they thought they'd covered everything. They qualified. They presented. They addressed concerns. But the client didn't buy.

In analyzing these past performances, nearly every salesperson came up with at least one situation in which they didn't really come right out and ask for the sale. If this has happened to you, chalk it up to inexperience, but don't let it happen again. Vow to never leave a client again without clearly asking for whatever it is you need to consider the sale closed: her approval on your paperwork; her purchase order number; or her money.

Chapter 15

Ten Ways to Put Your Clients at Ease

. . . .

. . . .

*W*hen you're a sales professional, you are in selling situations several times a day, every day — at least that's the way it should be if you're planning to earn much of an income. So sooner or later, being in these situations becomes comfortable to you. Not so for your clients (unless you work strictly with purchasing agents). For most customers, the thought of being involved in a selling situation ranks right up there with having a root canal done. They'll put it off as long as possible and then dread it when they finally have to come in and talk to you. Your clients will be uncomfortable, which is why one of your goals is to do everything in your power to make them comfortable before you ask for the final decision.

Be Friendly, Trustworthy, and Smart

Your first goal with people is to make them like you, trust you, and want to listen to you. Accomplish this by being friendly, warm, and open. You need to come across with an attitude of:

✔ "I'm here to help you."

✔ "Your needs are important to me."

✔ "I want to help you find a solution that's truly good for you."

After people realize that you're sincere, they relax and start talking with you. They start to trust you. Demonstrate your expertise on your product or service by answering their questions. Encourage your customers by asking questions about the who, what, when, where, and why of their situation.

Show Genuine Interest in the Customer

People the world over are flattered when others show interest in them; this makes them feel important. Your customers may get warm fuzzies inside to think that you think enough of them to show interest. Warm fuzzies are good. Don't ask only about things related to the product or service. Follow their lead and ask about their families, where they live, and other general interest questions that show you're human — and not just a lean, mean, selling machine. However, be prepared to take control if the conversation gets too long or too far off base. If this happens, gently bring the customers back to the topic at hand: their needs and how your product will satisfy them.

Be a Good Host

If you sell swimming pools in the desert, it's always a good idea to offer a cold drink to people who come to take a look at your pool display. Doing so is not only a nice courtesy, it's also an excellent way to get the customer envisioning herself hanging out by the pool, sipping a cool drink on a hot day. Make your customers comfortable. If you sell snowblowers, try offering coffee or hot cocoa. This is a great way to put the prospect in mind of the type of day she'll need to use that snowblower.

If you offer the refreshment in a glass or mug that isn't disposable, the customer will feel obligated to stay at your location until she finishes it — which guarantees you more time to do your sales pitch. Don't hand the customer a can of soda that she can walk away with; she may just take it with her over to the competition. If your client is a qualified buyer, the longer the amount of time she spends with you, the more likely she'll buy from you.

Keep the Kids Busy

If your customers have children with them, be sure to ask the children's names and shake their hands. Treat them as being important to the buying decision. Then keep your eye on them.

If the kids start to distract the parents from the selling situation, get them busy. Having coloring books and crayons on hand is always a good idea. Many retail stores have kids' corners filled with Legos, books, and sometimes even a VCR with a popular movie or cartoon playing. The reason for this is simple: The parents will spend more time (maybe even more than they originally planned) if they can make their decisions without interruptions or a sense of urgency to get going because the kids are bored. Do whatever it takes to allow the decision makers to focus on the task at hand.

Get the Customer Physically and Mentally Involved

The first time you attempt anything, you're a bit uncomfortable with it, right? Of course. Understanding that, realize that your clients will be uncomfortable the first time they have to use the new copier, drive the new car, or figure out the new investment portfolio report. To overcome this fear of the unknown — a fear that can prevent your prospects from making a buying decision — you have to get them physically and mentally involved in your product or service before you can consider asking for their decision. Involve the customers by handing them things — let them touch and feel the product to become more familiar with it:

> ✔ Let them punch the buttons.

> ✔ Have them turn the windshield wipers on and off and adjust the seats and mirrors.

> ✔ Walk them through simple calculations.

For intangibles:

> ✔ Let them handle charts and graphs.

> ✔ Help them see themselves relaxing instead of cleaning house.

In other words, allow your customers to get a taste of ownership of your product or service during the entire presentation. Who knows, maybe they won't want to give that diamond bracelet back after the lovely lady has tried it on and the gentleman has seen the new sparkle it brings to her eyes. Get the customers involved!

Eliminate Distractions

I talk about handling kids earlier in the chapter. Another distraction can come in the form of noise from telephones and other people's conversations. If at all possible, comfortably seat your prospects in an area away from anything that may take their focus off your presentation. If you're in the client's office, suggest she hold her calls and close the door. Move to a conference room if need be. You may want to enlist the aid of a secretary in setting up a few moments of peace.

Beware of personal distractions. A good way to check and make sure that you yourself are not a distraction is to videotape yourself rehearsing a presentation or else ask someone you trust to watch you while you rehearse. Some common distractions are

- ✔ Unusual hand gestures or using exaggerated facial expressions.
- ✔ Wearing too much jewelry.
- ✔ Extremely bold clothing (color or otherwise).
- ✔ Carrying too much stuff.

Streamlining is a good practice to develop when preparing to do business with the general public. If you don't need your whole briefcase and your DayTimer and your pager and your cellular phone for the 20 minutes you'll spend with the customer, leave them in the car.

The less stuff you have with you, the fewer distractions you will cause.

Use Body Language

If your body language sends a message that you're anxious, nervous, or that you have dollar signs in your eyes when you look at the prospective client, you lessen your chances of ever making a sale. Here are a couple of body language signals to avoid:

- ✔ **Open-palm hand gestures:** The message may come across that you're pushing the customer away from you.
- ✔ **Leaning too far forward or standing too close:** This action cramps the customer's personal space, making her uncomfortable.

Use what you learn about body language to make changes now — and avoid losing sales later.

Chapter 2 is full of information on body language.

Do a Summary Review for the Customer

Many people don't really know just what they want or need when shopping. Making a buying decision is a process of consideration and elimination. You, the sales professional, need to talk to the customer about her needs and then offer the options available to her, applying appropriate weight or value to each option that comes up. After sifting or boiling down the many aspects of products and services, people are then usually ready to make decisions, but will often hesitate because they're not 100 percent certain that they've covered all their concerns.

The best way to handle this uncertainty is to jot down notes as you go along on your sales journey with the customer. When you feel you're close to decision time, you can use your notes to step back and review the big picture — everywhere you've been in your presentation.

> We discussed the various colors and chose Desert Rose because it will look best with the fabric you have chosen for your sofa. We selected three styles of chairs considering your overall look, and you're certain the wing chair has the look you want. You've considered three types of wood for the tables and I think we've agreed that the oak with a light stain would brighten the room. Does all of this sound about right to you?

If you've taken good notes, the customer will be nodding all through your summary. When she reviews her thoughts and feelings over each decision and agrees that you've got it right, you're only a couple inches of ink away from closing the sale.

The more complicated the sale, the more important the summary review is. A summary review eliminates all the ancillary discussion and gets the final decision down to the nuts and bolts. (However, a summary review is still important with a simple or small sale.)

Slow Down the Pace

For most people, when they get close to making a decision that requires them to separate themselves from their money, they tend to get nervous. The client may dig in her heels. She may feel rushed or even panicky. And the closer the customer gets to making a decision, the more fears come to the surface. This tendency may be a remnant of our survival instinct to fight or flee when experiencing fear. The point here is that it's a natural occurrence for the customer to feel nervous and there's not much you can do to prevent it. So expect it and do what it takes to make the customer relax.

The best course of action is to simply slow things down a bit — let the panic subside. So what if she makes the decision in ten minutes instead of right this second? If you're pretty sure that the client is going to make the purchase, giving her a bit of breathing space can be the best thing you can do. If you're not sure, then it's time for a test close or summary review. If you decide you need to give your customer some space, here are some ways to do just that:

- ✔ Briefly excuse yourself and step away.

- ✔ Change the subject.

- ✔ Bring some humor into the conversation.

- ✔ Do something that makes the customer feel less pressured — even if it means point-blank apologizing for making her feel pressured.

> Let me apologize for my zealousness. I didn't mean to move so rapidly. I know you still have some questions regarding this decision, so let's slow things down a bit and cover them.

- ✔ Run through another summary review (see the earlier section "Do a Summary Review for the Customer"). This may help get the customer back on track and focused on all the good things about your product.

Take Yourself out of the Picture

Car salespeople have the right idea in this area. When buyers seem uncomfortable with the negotiations, the car salesperson will often offer to go to the sales manager to see if he can arrange a better investment or terms. By doing this, the salesperson places himself as the good guy, putting distance between himself and the negotiation process — he's working in the buyers' best interest. If the sale goes through, the salesperson is the hero for going to bat for the client. If the sale doesn't happen, the customers don't hold it against the car salesman; the blame can fall on the absent sales manager.

Chapter 16

The Ten Biggest Closing Mistakes

· ·

In This Chapter

▶ Gaining insight into the little things that could be holding you back

▶ Becoming absolutely certain that you've asked for the sale

· ·

A common mistake among salespeople is failing to identify common mistakes and then planning methods to overcome them. It stands to reason that you can't fix what you don't see as broken. This chapter covers the ten biggest closing mistakes that everyone makes — and they shouldn't be eye-openers. Instead, reading through this chapter should have you nodding your head and relating. If you find yourself reading something that you weren't aware of, make note of it to avoid potential closing challenges.

If you discover that you're making some or all of these common closing mistakes, don't take it too hard; you're in good company. For best results though, focus on one or two issues at a time. What is it they say about Rome not being built in a day? As you get better at one, move on to one or two more. Be warned: You may find yourself slipping back into old habits; at that point, you need to backtrack and refresh yourself. The more aware you are of your closing mistakes, the better sales closer you'll become.

The following ten mistakes are in no special order — they are all of equal importance and any one of them can bring a successful close to a standstill. Some of the closing mistakes are easier to identify than others, but that doesn't necessarily make them easier to resolve or correct. (And sometimes the easier the mistake is to correct, the easier it is to forget about it, too.) So take these items a few at a time, study them, and make a commitment to become a better closer.

Not Asking for the Business

You'd think it would be clear whether or not you've actually asked for the business, wouldn't you? Not so! Opinion questions are often confused with closing questions. Take a look at this example and ask yourself if this is a close or just a question that asked for an opinion.

> So how do you feel about being the owner of this beautiful, red sports car today?

Sounds like a close, but it really isn't. All you've done is ask for the customer's opinion, his feelings. Maybe he'd feel great about owning that new car today, but is it going to happen?

On the other hand, I've heard some salespeople say something like this:

> What can I do today that would help you drive home in this beautiful car?

Is this a closing question? Well, this is a test close (see Chapter 5), but still not a close. The prospect is probably going to list some things he needs to make his decision, but he still hasn't been asked a clear closing question. And although "Are you buying this car or not?" is a closing question, it's not one that will often lead to a close. So how do you ask, know that you've asked, and feel confident that you haven't worded the question too forcefully or too vaguely? To avoid ambiguity in your closing situations, be sure to do the following:

✔ Go back and review your notes. Go right down the list with the customer about all the things he said he was looking for in a new car. (I talk more about summary reviews in Chapter 15.)

✔ Point out the extra benefits he'll receive by purchasing the product from *your* company — not just any company.

✔ Conjure positive emotions by painting a picture of how the customer will feel when using his new product.

✔ Talk about the price and show that the product is within the prospect's budget. In fact, you may be able to get him excited about the price of the product being a bit lower than he had anticipated.

After you do all of this and do it well, the close may be as simple as handing the customer the paperwork and pen and saying, "Here!"

Giving Away Too Much Too Soon

Salespeople who rely on discounting the price to close the sale end up giving away the farm to harvest one crop. Think of the close as harvesting your fees for service:

✔ You worked hard to plant the seeds of need.

✔ You cultivated the land with targeted questioning strategies.

✔ You nurtured the seedlings with a presentation filled with enthusiasm and information.

Then, just about the time you're ready to harvest your crop, a severe storm comes up. What do you do? Instead of waiting until morning to see what damage is done and what you can salvage (because you're a great farmer whose knowledge of the soil and tended crop can right almost any wrong), you sell the farm for a one-time, rock-bottom price and move on.

See how appropriate this analogy is? Salespeople "sell the farm" in desperation all the time. Deep down they know what it will take to make the close, but they don't hang in there for the duration. They either try to close too soon by taking shortcuts that only make customers feel pressured and rushed, or else they think the way to overcome an objection is to simply offer more of a discount. (Not to say that a discount won't help to push the close over the edge now and then, but it isn't the only way — and it's not usually the preferable way to close a transaction, either.) The best way to close is to:

1. **Build rapport**

2. **Question**

3. **Present**

4. **Address concerns**

5. **Question some more**

6. **Test close**

7. **Address any final concerns**

8. **Close!**

Get the picture? Closing a sale is a back-and-forth, ongoing process that requires all parties to want to do business together more than they want to give up and walk out the door.

The biggest reason that salespeople discount early is that they haven't built up the value of their product or service. When customers first ask about discounts, a top closer reiterates the total value and helps the customer understand the value they'll receive by investing in the product or service, thereby getting a customer to *not* expect a discount.

Closing can also take a lot of energy. Some salespeople give away too much too soon because they want to get this difficult close over with and move on to something easier, which is laziness on their part. This type of salesperson isn't prepared to face five "Nos" before getting a "Yes," so they give up before there's time for a successful close. As a salesperson, you need to know what it takes to be a superstar in your profession and refuse to settle for anything less. If being a superstar means working that extra hour every day, do it with anticipation of the payoff for your hard work. If it means making one more call when your feet are falling off, make the call with a positive attitude. Go the extra mile to close the sale — don't give up.

Most of all, be patient with the selling process. It's Murphy's Law that just after you give away the farm, the customer will say, "Oh, I'm thrilled that you discounted the price, but I was really more concerned about the monthly terms of the lease!" Don't give away too much too soon. Zip your lip and wait for your prospects to come to a decision.

Nonstop Talk — Shut Up and Close

Another common closing mistake is nonstop talking. If you're not willing to close your mouth and wait for the customer to make a decision, it's going to cost you. Whoever said talk is cheap is wrong in this case. Talk is very, very expensive. After your presentation, stop talking and wait for your customer to talk. Otherwise, you may cost yourself a sale. Keep this in mind to help you remember: The first one to talk after a closing question loses!

When your customer says yes, don't keep talking. Get the paperwork authorized and leave as soon as you can (but not so fast that you look like a qualifier for the 100-yard dash). The longer you stay, the more you'll be tempted to talk. And the more you talk, the greater the chance of inadvertently introducing an objection to the sale.

Just Not in the Mood to Sell

Oftentimes salespeople feel like they have to be "on" — on establishing rapport; on asking targeted questions; on making their presentation. They are on almost all the time, which can be the fun part of selling. But there are some days when being on requires more than you have to give. Maybe you're just not in the mood to see people, and the focus required to make the close is more than you can muster.

If this is an accurate picture of your current career — on a daily basis — you may be in trouble. You may want to consider changing companies or professions. However, if you are just occasionally intolerant of your profession, there are some things you can do to pull yourself out of your funk. Find what motivates you — whether it's music, a motivational tape, talking with your manager, or whatever — and get on it! Then, get back to work.

Another way to get back in the groove is to motivate yourself by motivating someone else, namely your customer. Sometimes the best inspiration can be found in seeing someone else doing well. All it takes is one great presentation to give you back your closing momentum. So make up your mind that the next person to walk through your door will get the most spectacular presentation he's ever heard. (This is usually not too difficult for most salespeople, as the presentation is their favorite part of the selling process.)

One option you may have that would greatly help this I'm-not-in-the-mood kind of day is to make arrangements to switch days off with another salesperson — if it's okay with your manager. Be honest with your coworker and manager about why you want to switch. If you don't make a habit of taking advantage of personal time off, they'll appreciate your honesty and try to accommodate your request. If you can't get the entire day off, sometimes a few extra minutes at lunch to walk around the block or read an article in your favorite magazine is enough to lift your mood.

Then, of course, are the days you can't change your situation or your mood, and those are the times when it's best to just grin and bear it. Most careers have a negative here and there; a negative in a salesperson's career is having to be up when you're feeling down. So how do you get up? Force yourself. Think about it: Most of your customers have never seen you before, or if they have, they don't know you well enough to know when you are faking a positive attitude. So fake it!

The best thing about faking a positive mental attitude is that the longer you fake it, the more positive you actually begin to feel. Instead, you find yourself listening and enjoying the selling process once again. Enjoy more — make more! Success in one area brings success in another, and there's nothing more effective for an attitude adjustment than a successful close.

Not Treating Each Sale Like a New Day

The best way to close is to treat each close as if it were your first big sale. Wouldn't that be a great way to sell? Remember the enthusiasm you had when you first started selling? What if you could have all the knowledge you have now and still have the enthusiasm of a brand new salesperson? Unbeatable! Such an incredible combination would guarantee a successful close.

The best way to achieve this combination is to treat each close as if it were a new day, a new opportunity to succeed. In other words, don't let your past experiences spill over and affect your future closings. And it doesn't matter if those past experiences were positive or negative; either way, they can hinder your ability to close the next transaction. Drop your negative baggage at the prospect's door or leave it in your trunk. Don't bring it into the room with a potential sale! While most people don't think of such a thing as *positive baggage,* a recent success can tend to make you too cocky.

Maintain an attitude of dedication to your career and remain determined to have the best year ever. Avoid too much play and/or too much panic when you've closed or not closed a sale.

Rushing the Close

When you read the phrase "rushing the close," do you think of yourself trying to take shortcuts? Or do you think of having to cut your presentation short because the person you were meeting with made another commitment? You need to first determine your perspective, and then figure out what to do to stop being rushed.

Take a look at the shortcut problem. Even the most seasoned salespeople take repeated shortcuts. Shortcuts are a bad idea and end up getting the better of you in the long run. The problem with the long run is that it's so much easier to think in terms of right now. It's so easy to say, "Rapport building? I don't really have to focus on building rapport. After all, we've talked on the phone quite often and already know the things we have in common." This is a bad attitude to have. You're taking a shortcut that rushes the close and can cost you the sale.

Suppose your customers are asking a lot of questions and look like they're excited about owning your product before you've had the opportunity to ask them a few important qualifying questions. Should you rush right through the qualifying and move to the close? Some salespeople do, and sometimes it works well — if the customers are really displaying buying signals, that is. If they're just having a great day and happy to be out and about on a Saturday afternoon and you rush them to the close because you think they're eager to own, you may pressure them right out the door.

And then there's the person with limited time. Say, for example, that you've made an appointment with the CEO of a large company. You've waited to see the prospect for two months and planned a dynamite 45-minute presentation. Within the first moment after entering his office, the CEO informs you that there has been a change in his schedule and you have only 15 minutes to complete the presentation. Rather than schedule another appointment that would give you sufficient time to make the presentation, you try to rush through it in 15 minutes. What happens? No time to build rapport; no time to ask questions; no time to present; and definitely no time to close!

When you rush the close, your customers feel rushed as well. Instead, be relaxed. Speak and move naturally. Be excited without bouncing off the walls. Act the same leading up to your close as you were when you were building rapport. There should be no change in the pattern or speed of your presentation, and there should be no nervous habits or signs. What there should be is a natural progression to a successful close. You practiced all the success strategies, made your customers comfortable during the process, and now you're ready to make the successful close.

Don't sabotage a good close by rushing.

Emphasizing the Logical Aspects Rather Than the Emotional

The close is an emotional build. In Chapter 1, I define closing as a symphony of words and phrases that emotionally build, culminating with a win-win final agreement. The music of the sale builds and builds and builds until emotions are high. But what about logic? Logic must be present — a player in the selling game — but not the main character. Build the emotions and leave it up to the customer to logically justify the purchase.

Don't forget to use emotion-building words and actions. Laughter is a great tool for building emotion. Positive words like "spectacular" or "romantic" may be just the right touch to help your customer picture himself owning your product. Attentive actions while listening to customer concerns is an excellent way to encourage customers to express and build emotions. Other actions, such as nodding your head and leaning forward in your chair, signal your concern for the customer and your desire to make him happy with your product or service.

Beware of using too much emotion and not enough logic. If a customer can't rationalize his decision to own your product or service after he's been emotionally hooked, you'll find yourself with cancelled sales.

Too Many Distractions

One of the biggest and most unresolved closing mistakes is when the success of the sale is prevented because of distractions, too many distractions, to build any kind of momentum toward a mutually beneficial close. Salespeople who go into the homes of their customers have the television, radio, telephone, fax, children, and pets to contend with. If the distractions hit you in the face — literally or figuratively — as you enter the home, there's probably no way you can continue without asking your customers to do something about the distractions. Or maybe you can rearrange your appointment for another location with fewer distractions.

So what about when you enter the home and the distractions don't seem too bad? Oftentimes, you enter a home and the television is on at a low volume so it doesn't seem like such a distraction. But then about the time you start to speak, you have a dog that wants out or in, a child that needs some help with her homework, or a ringing phone that can't be ignored. Every good salesperson knows that every distraction during a presentation requires review to get back to the spot where you were before. With multiple distractions, all you're doing is backtracking.

You also have to deal with inner distractions, which can take on a variety of forms. Maybe you just had an argument with your teenager — and now you're expected to put all that behind you. Or perhaps you've had an incredibly great week and all you can think about is going to happy hour on Friday night and celebrating your success.

Another inner distraction on the part of the salesperson is the internal dialogue that makes him or her feel inadequate or self-conscious. With all the talk going on inside your head, how in the world can you expect to concentrate on the conversations going on outside your head? That's right — you can't. The best thing a salesperson can do is make sure his or her personal life is rewarding. Talk about a sales boost! Conversely, if your life is not balanced, your closing volume will show that.

The way to handle all these distractions is to stop entertaining them — both inside and out. If the selling circumstances aren't conducive to success, rearrange the circumstances to your liking. If you can't get your mother's recent illness out of your head, pay her a visit or make a phone call so you can free up your mind to continue your work. In this day and age, salespeople really have to work to rid themselves of all the distractions.

Keep this little tidbit in mind: Big distractions equal big killers to the close!

You're Not in Control

When you lose control of the selling situation, you lose control of the ability to close. But there is a way around this: Prepare for every situation you can think of. Being prepared doesn't mean that you won't have some unexpected surprises, but it does mean that you're ready to handle the situation. In other words, you're in control. Your customer won't be able to fire one unanswerable question after another and leave you holding the bag. Instead, if you're prepared for every possible objection you can think of, you'll be quick with answers to their concerns.

How do you take charge? Decide ahead of time on what you want to happen during the selling situation. Decide how and when you'll close. And then prepare your questions and answers.

Questions help you keep control. (Check out Chapter 5 for more on this.)

Go through the selling scenario several times before you actually make a call or welcome customers through your front door. Know the answers you want to receive; then design questions to get your customers to give you those answers. Decide what you will offer them and stay committed. Depend on your selling skills to close the sale instead of giving in to the demands of customers. You are not the puppet of your customers — and most won't respect you if you act like one. Take charge of the situation.

Knowing where you want to go and then leading the conversations and negotiations toward that goal makes you a leader. An excellent leader doesn't have trouble finding followers. Establish control by doing what's best for your customers, and they'll gladly give you control in the situation. If you were a brain surgeon, would you let your patients tell you how to operate? If you were a pilot, would you let your passengers fly the plane? I certainly hope not! You are a professional — a professional salesperson. Believe in yourself and so will your customers. Know that you are the expert and conduct yourself accordingly. Being the expert means taking responsibility of the selling situation and therefore controlling the outcome.

Prejudging a Prospect's Ability to Own

Here are two general rules to follow when it comes to sales: Never make a judgment on whether your customer can afford or will want your product, and always assume that they can afford it and do want it. Then begin the questioning and qualifying process. Until you discover otherwise, that customer facing you is your most able and willing owner.

Not all qualified owners look "qualified." Isn't it reasonable to believe that rich people dress in cutoffs and tennis shoes every once in awhile? And wouldn't you agree that many people who can't afford the jewelry at Tiffany's still go to the store to window shop? As the salesperson, you must never prejudge one way or another, but instead assume everyone shopping in your store is the next proud owner of your one-of-a-kind product — even if it's a $100,000 diamond ring.

Chapter 17

Ten Ideas for Creative Closing

*T*oday's customers are more sophisticated than ever. They've been exposed to advertising and marketing plans, and they've learned to be somewhat savvy in many respects and somewhat jaded in others. Your customers are likely to see the close coming in most selling situations. They know when they're being closed, and it's not a feeling they particularly like. So for you to stand out above the crowd — to become the champion salesperson you want to become — you need to seek out creative ways to close sales.

Observe How Children Close

Children are born with a natural talent to get what they want, to persuade, to convince. Kids in action are a wonder to watch because they've got their closing technique down pat and are experts when it comes to persuasion and convincing others to their way of thinking. One of the best models of a champion closer may be in your very own children. (If you're not a parent, don't skip this part. Simply borrow somebody else's kids for awhile and observe their creative methods of closing.)

Look back on the last time you noticed that a child wanted something and knew the only way she was going to get it was to convince her parents that it was a great idea. I've seen children persuade a parent who hated reptiles into buying the child not one, but two, and then agree to put out the money to buy food for the new pet every week. I've also seen a teenager cleverly convince her parents that she needed a car. She presented her plight in such a touching manner that it was difficult for her parents to say no. She was entering her first year of college at an out-of-state university and knew that her parents wouldn't want her to be out walking the streets late at night in a strange city. She was a natural closer.

What children do better than most adult closers is target the concerns of those they are trying to convince to their way of thinking. Obviously, children already know the beliefs and concerns of their parents, so they hit hard the areas that are most emotionally persuasive. If a parent is concerned about the safety of his child, the child will work out a way to focus on the added safety of getting what he wants. I've seen a kid do this with a video game — and that's a stretch. The clever child pointed out that he would be safer owning this video game because he wouldn't have to hang around the video game room where kids could pick fights with him and possibly steal his money. Another excellent close. Watch and learn from kids; they are masters at closing.

Observe How Pets — That's Right, Pets — Close

If you have a pet, you know exactly what we're talking about. I'm going to focus on dogs here because they are outstanding closers. (Not to neglect other pets you may have, but for this case, a dog is a perfect example.) Dogs play the adorable role. They get what they want by having the best relationship with you and always forgiving your bad moods or inattentive nature. When you come home from work, they're always there to greet you with enthusiasm and excitement. When they're this cheerful, how can you refuse them a small little treat or a walk around the neighborhood?

The expression "puppy dog eyes" didn't come out of nowhere. A dog knows how to make great eye contact. Have you ever noticed how a dog will not take his eyes off you when he wants something? If you're eating, the dog watches every tasty morsel travel to your mouth. If the adorable expression doesn't sway you, the guilt certainly will.

 You can use these strategies with potential clients: Be an excellent listener; let the customers know you're there for them; make great eye contact; and sense their mood by watching body language.

Okay, just to be fair to all those other pets out there, every pet has a different method of persuasion. A cat will withhold affection until you give in. A bird will not shut up until you let it out of its cage. I've even heard of a fish spitting water out of the tank until its owner came with the food. That's closing, folks! (Of course, you shouldn't spit at your customers. The key here is that persistence pays.)

Take a Cue from Health Care Professionals

Doctors are closers — and I'm not talking about stitches here. Doctors and other health care professionals take a different approach to closing, though; they expect success because of their expertise. After all, that's why the patient is there. You never hear a doctor say, "Please, please, please get this operation!" Doctors rely on their reputation of being the most knowledgeable in the field. They are the expert advisors, so they know they'll make the close with their "client." The point here is that people rarely question those they believe to be in authority. A person believes that doctors know what they're doing, so few challenge their opinions. At most, all they'll do is ask for a second opinion from another doctor.

Your mission is to watch your health care professionals for their style, their air of authority, and how they demonstrate their expertise. After observing, put what you've learned into practice in your field. After people believe that you're the best expert in town on your product or service, they'll not only become clients, they'll send you their friends, family members, and acquaintances, too.

Take Advantage of Professionally Produced Training

There are tons of books in libraries about selling techniques, but you have to be aware of one simple, often ignored detail: Some of the authors have never sold anything in their lives except the very book you are reading or the tapes you're listening to. Be selective in who you study. Find out who are good closers in real-life sales and then adopt some of their teachings. Also, don't look at just one source. Examine the differences in a variety of top closers' methods. Pick a little here and there to incorporate into your own original and creative method of closing. When you study the greats, don't just listen to ways they tell you to close — try to see them in action. For example, if you're attending a seminar, watch how they close you on their products. Are they practicing what they preach? Were you persuaded to own?

Keep a Journal of Interesting Closing Strategies

A journal can be an invaluable tool for becoming a master closer. I would venture to say that most superstar closers have forgotten more creative methods of closing than the average salesperson ever learns. So listen to top producers in your sales meetings when they talk about a particular closing situation and write down how they handled it. If they simply describe the situation, be proactive and ask them for the wording they used.

The great thing about keeping a journal is that you can look over it at your leisure. I've even heard of some salespeople taping great closes so they can listen to them in their car on the way to an especially difficult meeting. By listening to the closing methods immediately before the meeting, the strategies are fresh in their minds and they are able to utilize the methods more readily.

You may want to categorize your closings notes. For example, keep all your standard closes in one area of your journal and all your humorous and creative ones in another section. Okay, that may be a bit retentive, but categorization makes it easier to search for the one close that may work with a particular type of customer or prospect. If you know your prospect is rather analytical, you may want to use a close that uses a lot of facts and information — an informative close. If your prospect is a talker, you may want to simply shut up and let them close themselves — think of this as the non-close close!

The more you talk to other good closers, the more you learn about closing. Good closers love to flaunt the fact that they can close. Listen to what they've tried, what worked, and what didn't. If anything, you'll enjoy the stories, and the closing information you gather will be incredibly valuable to your future closing situations. Encourage other salespeople you know to talk about closing situations. Ask their opinion on a particular type of close that didn't work as you thought it would. And be willing to share stories of your own about a way you closed that brought you unexpected success.

One of the great things about being a salesperson is the friends you make and the camaraderie you share with others who share similar experiences; it's like being in a giant sales club, and you've got the inside track on what makes the world go 'round. Selling is an exciting environment; use that excitement to become a better closer.

Watch the News

At our Academy of Master Closing three-day seminars, we give our students a homework assignment every night. On the second night, their assignment is to find something in a magazine, newspaper, or from the radio or television news — in other words, something topical — that can be used in a close. You may think this a daunting task; however, our Academy students have already completed two days of intense study with us by the time they receive this assignment. (By the way, our staff, myself included, undertakes this same assignment so we're prepared to prove it can be done.) It's amazing what you find when your mind is committed to a particular task:

- ✔ During Desert Storm, we found wonderful military strategies to use as analogies for decision making with clients. For example, the Colin Powell close in Chapter 7 was derived from something this great military leader said. We probably wouldn't have heard his message if it weren't for Desert Storm.

- ✔ Most people have some sort of sports loyalty. If you know your client's favorite team, read about them. Look for quotes from the players or coaches. Share your client's interest and use this to foster a bond.

- ✔ Crime stories can help you move security products.

- ✔ Accidents that make the news help sell insurance.

- ✔ Medical breakthroughs and technological advancements help you show your prospects how fast the world is changing. The speed of change can be turned into a close because it prompts the customer into action.

Put a New Twist on the Proven Standards

Although new and creative closes are fun to try, don't forget to continue to use the closes that have worked for years. You don't have to reinvent the wheel, but you sure can try a new tread on it. I've revised and reworked nearly all the closes that I learned from my mentor, J. Douglas Edwards, to keep them current with today's marketplace. The foundation for each of the closes was sound — I just adapted them to keep them fresh. Some of the closes I developed early in my career still work today, but I've changed the phraseology to be less formal as our daily exchanges have become less formal. As long as you don't change the basic psychology behind the closes (helping your customers overcome fear, or indecision, or procrastination, and so on), you'll be all right.

Ask Your Clients about Their Most Interesting Closes

You may think I've gone mad, but I promise you I haven't. Think about those clients with whom you have a good relationship. They probably make more buying decisions than just the one involving your product, which means that they talk with a lot of sales professionals in different fields. Ask them about a recent purchase they've made (other than yours) and what made them choose that particular company to work with. Ask how the salesperson persuaded them to own his product. Explain to your customers that you're asking because you're always trying to learn more and improve your sales skills.

Don't use the same close the clients shared with you the next time they come in. However, it may be a great one for your next potential client.

Use Your Imagination

Dream up scenarios — and not just those where the client says, "Where do I sign?" Imagine the sale of a lifetime with a tough negotiator.

- ✔ What are all the things that could possibly come up?
- ✔ How would you handle them?

Create a close and then see if you can actually visualize yourself using the close. Sometimes your creativity may be better in thought than in practice. You may find yourself with a very creative close that you can never imagine yourself using. Continue to bend and twist your close until you find a way to put it into practice. And you thought daydreaming was a waste of time! Daydreaming can be highly productive. Just limit the time you spend daydreaming so that you don't miss out on real opportunities.

Something else you may want to consider when creating a new close is to practice it before you use it on your biggest account or your most important client. As with any skill, there's a learning curve — a time that you need to perfect your new method. Give yourself a few practice runs before you meet with the big boys! If an attempt to creatively close doesn't turn out exactly as expected, take time to make revisions, and then practice the new version before trying it out on your biggest account.

Chapter 18

Ten Ways to Master the Art of Closing

*I*f you don't love selling yet, follow these ten steps to mastering the closing skills presented in this book. I believe you'll find yourself loving selling more and more because you'll be serving more people and earning more money. The rewards will be tremendous!

Become a Student

I think you'd probably agree with me that it's tough to master a new skill if you have a mental block of some sort. The mental block may be that you don't like feeling uncomfortable, and mastering new things makes you experience a certain degree of discomfort. Or maybe the mental block is that you think you already know a good bit about the subject and don't really have much more to learn. (The sign of true professionals, however, is how much they can learn after they know it all.) Your mental block may be any number of things, but you have to get past them to become a master closer.

In order to take the first uncomfortable steps of figuring out something new, you have to commit to becoming a student. You have to put on your thinking cap. You may have to take notes. You have to read. You even have to memorize some things. Take yourself back to your school days and remember how it felt to be a student in your favorite class. You couldn't wait for class. You may have even read ahead in the textbook. You listened attentively. You took great notes and thoroughly enjoyed talking with others about the subject of interest. If you adopt that attitude with mastering the material in this book, you'll achieve mastery much sooner that someone who takes it on as a burden.

Do the Most Productive Thing

After you've committed to learning the material, the next step is to set aside a specific time period, whether it's daily or weekly, to invest in study. When it comes to time planning, the best advice I ever received was to do the most productive thing possible at every given moment. Any time I found myself chatting with someone in the office, I'd cut it short by reminding myself that this person wasn't likely to list her home with me or send me buyers. The most productive thing for me to do was to serve the clients I already had or work on getting more clients.

Will it be more productive for you to invest the first hour of every day in making phone calls? Or is it better to review a few closing strategies before talking with clients? I recommend that a minimum of one hour per day, every day, be invested in improving your skills. Don't make exceptions for weekends or holidays. Make your continuing education a daily habit.

Whether you spend or invest your time is up to you.

Make Closing Your Hobby

Making your profession your hobby is how you fall in love with selling. Say your hobby is growing roses. How do you treat that hobby? You read about it. You may subscribe to a magazine about it. You may belong to a rose garden club. You attend rose shows. You may even enter your roses in competition. You spend time with your roses. You nurture them. Apply this same kind of time and attention to selling.

Start with this book. Keep it with you as much as possible. Read and review the material not only during your one hour of committed study time, but while you're waiting at stop lights. Read while you're standing in line. (Hey, it's more productive than just staring blankly at the menu board at your favorite burger joint.) Take the book in the bathroom with you, for Pete's sake. Highlight the material on each page that you feel is most pertinent to you. Use sticky notes to mark pages you refer to frequently. Write in the margins. Make this book look like last year's phone book. This book is not a library reference book that needs to be kept in immaculate condition for centuries. This book will do you good only if what's inside of it goes inside of you — and I don't mean to tear the pages out and put them between two slices of bread!

Then, go get another book — I suggest *Selling For Dummies* (IDG Books Worldwide, Inc.). Become more well-rounded in your selling career by gaining a clearer understanding of how to complete the other steps in the selling cycle in the most professional manner. Invest in audio cassettes and videos. Start a selling journal — a notebook in which you keep your best thoughts about selling, ideas for new closes, and motivational sayings that help you stay focused.

Turn sales closing into your hobby. Both you and your clients will have more fun in your selling situations, and you'll both reap more rewards than you ever thought possible.

Use Affirmations

I'm a firm believer in the power of affirmations. An *affirmation* is a positive statement that you choose to write for yourself, about yourself. Here are a couple of examples:

- ✔ I am good at closing sales because I have mastered the delivery of multiple closing strategies.
- ✔ I close a lot of sales because I sincerely care about serving the needs of my clients.

Just imagine how good you would be if those statements rang true. Well, they can be true. I suggest you write a series of not more than six affirmation statements. Then read them out loud to yourself several times each day. I suggest you do it in front of the mirror at home while looking yourself in the eye. You can also read them during various lulls in the day for a quick refresher. Most importantly, read them to yourself before you go to sleep at night. Your subconscious mind will accept them as true and work on whatever it takes to bring your affirmations to fruition.

See Yourself Succeeding

Before every appointment I had in the real estate business, I would sit in my car for a few moments and visualize myself walking out the front door of the home with an approved listing agreement in my hand. I would picture myself with potential buyers, shaking their hands and congratulating them on owning their new home.

Visualization strategies are used by great athletes. They picture themselves in top condition. They feel the wind in their hair or the water gliding over their bodies. They envision the power it takes to beat the competition. They see themselves on the platform, accepting the medal.

These strategies aren't reserved only for athletes. Top professionals in every endeavor use them. You can, too. Picture yourself winning with each prospective client. Picture yourself cashing bigger and bigger checks. See yourself winning top honors at the company awards ceremony. Why not? Seeing is believing. And when you truly believe you can accomplish something, the effort it takes to do it seems less strenuous.

P.D.R.

I drill these three letters into the minds of my students at our live seminars. I tell them, "If you want to succeed in selling, you must P.D.R. If you have a desire to earn a large income, you have to P.D.R. And if you want to achieve champion status in your field of endeavor, you must P.D.R." The letters P.D.R. stand for *Practice, Drill,* and *Rehearse.* You can't just read the closing material in this book. You can't just memorize it, either. You have to practice it. Drill it into your mind and then rehearse with a trusted associate, loved one, or in front of your mirror so you get the body language down. Master the appropriate gestures, not just the words. Your body language and gestures are as important as the words you say. So memorize the words, yes. But don't stop there. Drill until you can deliver your close naturally. Rehearse until you feel relaxed about your style.

Put Your Closes to Work

After you've completed the preceding items, the next thing to do is put all that you've learned into practice. Any performer can tell you that all the learning and all the rehearsal in the world won't earn you applause until you perform in front of a live audience. You won't earn any income from the material in this book until you use it with a living, breathing, qualified, potential client. I recommend that you commit 21 days to studying and rehearsing the material, and then commit the next 21 days to applying it.

Analyze Your Ability

During the application stage of mastery, you need to be particularly attentive to details. Pay close attention to both yourself and your client while delivering the new material:

- ✔ How did you move into the close?
- ✔ Was the close a smooth or rough transition?
- ✔ How did the client react?
- ✔ Did you close the sale?

If you did close the sale, wonderful. If you didn't make the close, what do you feel was missing?

Take a few minutes after every presentation and dissect what went right and what went wrong. Figure out how you can modify your method to make it even better. Masters are constantly tweaking and fine-tuning their abilities; they don't just master something, decide they've gone far enough, and stop learning. Self-analysis is critical to the achievement of greatness!

Keep Your Goals in Sight

What keeps you motivated? Hopefully your goals will. If you have clearly defined goals that are formed around your desire to become a selling champion, you'll find yourself motivated by your goals when the effort seems too much. If your goal is a family trip to Disneyland and you have to meet 105 percent of quota to get there, you'll find that this goal — along with your family — will inspire you if it all seems to be too much. Let others know what you're trying to accomplish — specifically loved ones or people who have something to gain when you do accomplish your goal. Let them help you. Rehearse with them. Ask their opinion of your delivery style. Get them involved.

I strongly recommend that you post your goals in your study area. If you have a designated area in your home where you study, line the walls with posters showing the goal you're striving to achieve. If your goal is something intangible, come up with words or phrases to describe it. Create an environment that will be highly conducive to your success.

If you know what you're going after and remind yourself of it constantly through visual images, you'll stay motivated to achieve when the going gets tough.

Don't Take Yourself Too Seriously

In the beginning, you're bound to screw up. How's that for positive thinking? Well, it's true. But don't let your initial failures get to you. Your attitude about this journey towards mastery will make a powerful impact on how long the journey is — or at least on how long the journey seems to take.

As I mention earlier in this chapter, you have to get uncomfortable before you can get comfortable with new material. Accept that fact, and you're halfway home. I've seen too many people stress out over not getting the material down pat the first time and get upset with themselves. There's no sense in making yourself miserable. Your learning abilities lessen under stress. Be willing to laugh at your mistakes as you learn. A little levity goes a long way. If you doubt that this is true, think about the last time you made a mistake. It probably wasn't too long afterward that you were recounting the tale to someone else and laughing about it. The key here is to laugh along the way while you're learning.

Index

● ●

• V •

• W •

• Y •

• Z •

FOR DUMMIES®

A world of resources to help you grow

HOME & BUSINESS COMPUTER BASICS

PCs FOR DUMMIES
0-7645-0838-5

The Flat-Screen iMac FOR DUMMIES
0-7645-1663-9

Windows XP ALL-IN-ONE DESK REFERENCE FOR DUMMIES
0-7645-1548-9

Also available:

Excel 2002 All-in-One Desk Reference For Dummies (0-7645-1794-5)

Office XP 9-in-1 Desk Reference For Dummies (0-7645-0819-9)

PCs All-in-One Desk Reference For Dummies (0-7645-0791-5)

Troubleshooting Your PC For Dummies (0-7645-1669-8)

Upgrading & Fixing PCs For Dummies (0-7645-1665-5)

Windows XP For Dummies (0-7645-0893-8)

Windows XP For Dummies Quick Reference (0-7645-0897-0)

Word 2002 For Dummies (0-7645-0839-3)

INTERNET & DIGITAL MEDIA

The Internet FOR DUMMIES
0-7645-0894-6

eBay FOR DUMMIES
0-7645-1642-6

Digital Photography FOR DUMMIES
0-7645-1664-7

Also available:

CD and DVD Recording For Dummies (0-7645-1627-2)

Digital Photography All-in-One Desk Reference For Dummies (0-7645-1800-3)

eBay For Dummies (0-7645-1642-6)

Genealogy Online For Dummies (0-7645-0807-5)

Internet All-in-One Desk Reference For Dummies (0-7645-1659-0)

Internet For Dummies Quick Reference (0-7645-1645-0)

Internet Privacy For Dummies (0-7645-0846-6)

Paint Shop Pro For Dummies (0-7645-2440-2)

Photo Retouching & Restoration For Dummies (0-7645-1662-0)

Photoshop Elements For Dummies (0-7645-1675-2)

Scanners For Dummies (0-7645-0783-4)

Get smart! Visit www.dummies.com

- **Find listings of even more Dummies titles**

- **Browse online articles, excerpts, and how-to's**

- **Sign up for daily or weekly e-mail tips**

- **Check out Dummies fitness videos and other products**

- **Order from our online bookstore**

FOR DUMMIES

Helping you expand your horizons and realize your potential

GRAPHICS & WEB SITE DEVELOPMENT

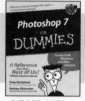

0-7645-1651-5

0-7645-1643-4

0-7645-0895-4

Also available:

Adobe Acrobat 5 PDF
For Dummies
(0-7645-1652-3)

ASP.NET For Dummies
(0-7645-0866-0)

ColdFusion MX for
Dummies
(0-7645-1672-8)

Dreamweaver MX For
Dummies
(0-7645-1630-2)

FrontPage 2002 For
Dummies
(0-7645-0821-0)

HTML 4 For Dummies
(0-7645-0723-0)

Illustrator 10 For
Dummies
(0-7645-3636-2)

PowerPoint 2002 For
Dummies
(0-7645-0817-2)

Web Design For Dummies
(0-7645-0823-7)

PROGRAMMING & DATABASES

0-7645-0746-X

0-7645-1626-4

0-7645-1657-4

Also available:

Access 2002 For Dummies
(0-7645-0818-0)

Beginning Programming
For Dummies
(0-7645-0835-0)

Crystal Reports 9 For
Dummies
(0-7645-1641-8)

Java & XML For Dummies
(0-7645-1658-2)

Java 2 For Dummies
(0-7645-0765-6)

JavaScript For Dummies
(0-7645-0633-1)

Oracle9i For Dummies
(0-7645-0880-6)

Perl For Dummies
(0-7645-0776-1)

PHP and MySQL For
Dummies
(0-7645-1650-7)

SQL For Dummies
(0-7645-0737-0)

Visual Basic .NET For
Dummies
(0-7645-0867-9)

LINUX, NETWORKING & CERTIFICATION

0-7645-1545-4

0-7645-1760-0

0-7645-0772-9

Also available:

A+ Certification For
Dummies
(0-7645-0812-1)

CCNP All-in-One
Certification For Dummies
(0-7645-1648-5)

Cisco Networking For
Dummies
(0-7645-1668-X)

CISSP For Dummies
(0-7645-1670-1)

CIW Foundations For
Dummies
(0-7645-1635-3)

Firewalls For Dummies
(0-7645-0884-9)

Home Networking For
Dummies
(0-7645-0857-1)

Red Hat Linux All-in-One
Desk Reference For
Dummies
(0-7645-2442-9)

UNIX For Dummies
(0-7645-0419-3)

Available wherever books are sold.
Go to www.dummies.com or call 1-877-762-2974 to order direct